Better Homes and Gardens®

CHRISTMAS

FROM THE HEART®

Volume 15

Meredith® Books
Des Moines, Iowa

Better Homes and Gardens

CHRISTMAS
FROM THE HEART

Editor: Jessica Saari
Contributing Editor: Carol Field Dahlstrom
Contributing Technical Writer: Susan M. Banker
Contributing Food Editor: Winifred Moranville
Assistant Art Director: Todd Emerson Hanson
Contributing Designer: Angie Haupert Hoogensen
Copy Chief: Terri Fredrickson
Publishing Operations Manager: Karen Schirm
Senior Editor, Asset and Information Manager: Phillip Morgan
Edit and Design Production Coordinator: Mary Lee Gavin
Editorial Assistant: Cheryl Eckert
Book Production Managers: Pam Kvitne,
    Marjorie J. Schenkelberg, Rick von Holdt, Mark Weaver
Contributing Copy Editor: Amy Spence
Contributing Proofreaders: Barb Rothfus, Judy Friedman,
    Karen Grossman
Cover Photographer: Pete Krumhardt
Photographers: Pete Krumhardt, Dean Tanner/Primary Image,
    Jay Wilde
Technical Illustrator: Chris Neubauer Graphics, Inc.
Project Designers: Kristin Detrick, Margaret Sindelar,
    Ann E. Smith, Jan Temeyer
Contributing Recipe Development: Joyce Lock
Photostyling Assistant: Donna Chesnut

Meredith® Books
Executive Director, Editorial: Gregory H. Kayko
Executive Director, Design: Matt Strelecki
Managing Editor: Amy Tincher-Durik
Senior Editor/Group Manager: Jan Miller
Senior Associate Design Director: Ken Carlson

Publisher and Editor in Chief: James D. Blume
Editorial Director: Linda Raglan Cunningham
Executive Director, Marketing: Steve Malone
Executive Director, New Business Development: Todd M. Davis
Executive Director, Sales: Ken Zagor
Director, Operations: George A. Susral
Director, Production: Douglas M. Johnston
Director, Marketing: Amy Nichols
Business Director: Jim Leonard

Vice President and General Manager: Douglas J. Guendel

Better Homes and Gardens® Magazine
Editor in Chief: Karol DeWulf Nickell
Deputy Editor, Food and Entertaining: Nancy Wall Hopkins
Senior Deputy Editor, Home Design: Oma Blaise Ford

Meredith Publishing Group
President: Jack Griffin
Executive Vice President: Bob Mate
Vice President, Corporate Solutions: Michael Brownstein
Vice President, Creative Services: Ellen de Lathouder
Vice President, Manufacturing: Bruce Heston
Vice President, Finance and Administration: Karla Jeffries
Vice President, Consumer Marketing: David Ball
Consumer Product Associate Marketing Director: Steve Swanson
Consumer Product Marketing Manager: Wendy Merical
Business Manager: Darren Tollefson
Consumer Marketing Director of Operations: Chuck Howell

Meredith Corporation
Chairman and Chief Executive Officer: William T. Kerr
President and Chief Operating Officer: Stephen M. Lacy

In Memoriam: E.T. Meredith III (1933-2003)

All of us at Meredith® Books are dedicated to providing you
with information and ideas to enhance your home. We welcome
your comments and suggestions. Write to us at: Meredith Books
Editorial Department, 1716 Locust St., Des Moines, IA
50309-3023. *Christmas From The Heart 2006* is available by mail.
To order editions from past years, call 800/627-5490.

Our seal assures you that every recipe in *Christmas
From The Heart 2006* has been tested in the
Better Homes and Gardens® Test Kitchen. This
means that each recipe is practical and reliable,
and meets our high standards of taste appeal.
We guarantee your satisfaction with this book
for as long as you own it.

Better Homes and Gardens®

CHRISTMAS

FROM THE HEART.

contents

perfectly plaid

Happy memories all come together on Christmas Eve. Lights twinkle and colors overlap creating the perfect holiday mood.

Blend color and texture in the colors of Christmas to create perfectly plaid patterned trims. To dress your Christmas tree with supersimple ribbon trims, **Plaid-Patch Ornaments**, *above*, do the trick. The snippets of plaid ribbon dancing on plain white bulbs lend a tailored, yet playful design. **The striking tree**, *opposite*, shows off even more spectacular plaid trims, which are shown in more detail on the following pages. Instructions for all of the ornaments are on *pages 16–18*.

These lovely ornaments include glorious symbols of the season. Holiday charms hang center stage in **Festive Frames**, *below left*. Shaped like Christmas trees, sparkling **Christmas Cones**, *below*, combine popular scrapbooking supplies. Keys seem to rekindle memories of home. May these **Christmas Keys**, *below right*, remind you of the love of family and friends as you hang each one. Shaped like stars and hearts, **Wooden Wonders**, *opposite*, lend rustic charm. **Beautifully Banded Ornaments**, *below far right*, take only seconds to make, so you can craft an extra batch to give as gifts. Instructions are on *pages 16–17*.

You'll love sharing **Wondrous Wishes**, *above*, on your holiday
tree. The dainty details look tricky to achieve, but only you
need to know that they are stickers. Extend your love for plaid
to your tabletop with a **Pretty Plaid Mat**, *opposite*. Quilted
from several plaid fabrics, the patched background sets off a
sprinkling of star motifs. Instructions are on *page 18*.

Master the art of ribbon weaving by crafting coordinating ornaments and stockings that sparkle with brilliant reds and greens. The **Plaid Pillow Trims**, *above*, are designed to make three at a time—multiplying the fun. For an heirloom in the making, a **Checkerboard-Cuff Stocking**, *opposite*, is just what Santa ordered. With a woven cuff and star design, this stocking begs to showcase a time-honored family brooch. Instructions are on *pages 18–21*.

Concentric circles fill the cuff of an **Adirondack
Stocking**, *above*, brightening up its simple plaid
base. Add to the project's vivid appeal by using
contrasting embroidery floss to stitch the circles in
place. On the coordinating **Adirondack Tree Skirt**,
opposite, tree motifs march around the five-square
design. Instructions are on *pages 20–23*.

perfectly plaid

Plaid-Patch Ornaments
shown on pages 6–7

WHAT YOU NEED
Scissors
Assorted thin plaid ribbon
White satin ornaments
Double-sided tape

HERE'S HOW
1 Cut small squares of ribbon and fray the ends using the tip of a scissors.
2 Adhere the ribbon pieces randomly to the ornaments using double-sided tape.

Christmas Cones
shown on pages 6 and 8

WHAT YOU NEED
Tracing paper; pencil
Scissors
Plaid scrapbook papers
Double-sided tape
3-D paint in glittering gold,
    such as Scribbles
Gold paint pen, optional
Small red marbles, optional
Small beads and/or marble assortment
    in gold, green, and red
Small box; ruler
20-gauge brass wire
Wire cutter
Round-nose pliers
Large glass beads in white, red,
    and green
½-inch sheer red ribbon

HERE'S HOW
1 Trace the pattern *below* onto tracing paper; cut out. Use the pattern to cut a pair of shapes from two contrasting scrapbook papers. Use double-sided tape to adhere the papers wrong sides together.
2 Use the gold paint pen or 3-D paint to outline the long curved edge of the paper that will be on the outside. If using 3-D

paint, sprinkle it with red marbles or the bead mixture.
3 Working in small sections, use 3-D paint to draw small rings, short lines, or other designs on the gold-edge side of the ornament. If desired just decorate the cone tip and edge. While the paint is wet, sprinkle with the bead mixture over a small box, allowing the excess to fall into the box. Continue working around the ornament until spotted with beaded areas. Let dry.
4 Shape the paper into a cone, overlapping the ends approximately 1 inch. Secure with double-sided tape.
5 Cut a 10-inch piece of wire. Use round-nose pliers to shape a tiny ring at one end. Slip a large bead on the straight end. Push the beaded wire up through the center of the ornament. Thread a red bead and a large green bead onto the wire, and coil the end.
6 Cut a 10-inch length of ribbon. Thread the ribbon through the wire coil. Knot the ribbon ends to secure.

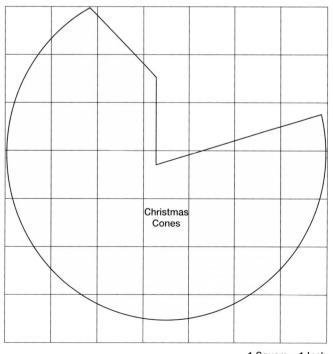

Christmas
Cones

1 Square = 1 Inch
Enlarge at 200%

Wooden Wonders

shown on pages 6 and 9

WHAT YOU NEED

Waxed paper
Wood hearts and stars
Inexpensive brush
Petroleum jelly, such as Vaseline
Acrylic paints in red and green
Putty knife
Newspapers
Clear varnish or top coat

HERE'S HOW

1 On a surface protected with waxed paper, lay out wood shapes and randomly brush small blotches of petroleum jelly onto the surfaces.

2 Brush one coat of acrylic green paint over the entire surface of each wood piece, gently painting over the top of the areas with petroleum jelly. Let painted pieces set for approximately 30 minutes.

3 Scrape the wood surface with a putty knife. Some original wood and some green paint will show. Again, randomly brush petroleum jelly onto the wood shapes. Cover the wood surfaces with red paint. Scrape the surface after 30 minutes to reveal some wood, green, and red areas.

4 In a well-ventilated work area, wipe any excess paint peelings. Cover the work surface with newspapers. Spray the surface with a clear varnish or top coat. Let dry.

Festive Frames

shown on pages 6 and 8

WHAT YOU NEED

Newspapers; wood decorative frames
Acrylic paints in white, red, and umber
Paintbrush
Soft rag; wire; wire cutter; ruler

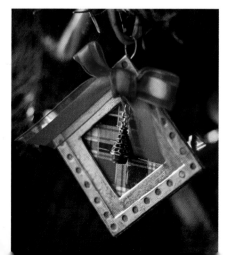

Holiday charms
Small jewelry chain, optional
Double-sided tape
Plaid scrapbook paper; scissors
Red ribbon

HERE'S HOW

1 Cover work surface with newspapers. Brush each frame with one coat of white paint. Let dry. Brush a light coat of red paint onto frame and immediately wipe it off while wet. Repeat the same procedure with the umber paint. Let dry.

2 Cut a 5-inch piece of wire and loop one end through the holiday charm. (Add a short length of jewelry chain to hang the charm lower if needed.) Bend the other end of wire and twist to form a loop for hanging the ornament. Cut off excess wire. Secure the wire and charm to a back corner of the frame using double-sided tape.

3 Cut out two squares of plaid paper slightly smaller than the outer edges of the frame. Tape the squares together, wrong sides facing each other. Adhere the paper pieces to the back of frame using double-sided tape.

4 Tie small ribbon bows and tape to the front of the frame.

Christmas Keys

shown on pages 6 and 9

WHAT YOU NEED

½-inch-wide plaid ribbons
Scissors; ruler; wire; wire snips
Vintage-look key
¼-inch-wide red satin ribbon
Scissors

HERE'S HOW

1 For each ornament, tie a bow using one of the plaid ribbons. Cut a 4-inch piece from a contrasting plaid ribbon and loop over the center of the bow.

2 Cut a 4-inch length of wire. Use the wire to secure the ribbons together, tightly wrapping twice just below the bow center.

3 Use the wire tails to secure the bow to the top of the key.

4 Cut a 12-inch length of red ribbon. Thread it through the loop in the key. Knot the ribbon ends together.

Beautifully Banded Ornaments

shown on pages 6 and 9

WHAT YOU NEED

Red satin ornaments
⅜-inch-wide plaid ribbon
Scissors
Double-sided tape
Ruler

HERE'S HOW

1 Using an ornament as a guide, cut a length of ribbon to wrap around the center of the ornament, allowing it to overlap ½ inch.

2 Adhere the ribbon to the ornament using double-sided tape.

3 Cut a 10-inch length of ribbon. Tie the ribbon to the ornament top, leaving a loop for hanging.

Wondrous Wishes

shown on pages 6 and 11

WHAT YOU NEED
Alphabet stickers
Scissors
Gold satin ornaments
Plaid stickers

HERE'S HOW

1 If necessary, trim area around alphabet stickers to allow stickers to lie flat on ornament's curved surface. Gently apply alphabet stickers horizontally or vertically to form words on ornament surface.

2 Cut thin short strips from plaid stickers and apply them as fringe around the top of the ornament.

Pretty Plaid Mat

shown on page 10

WHAT YOU NEED
Tracing paper; pencil
Yellow fabric scraps
Scissors
5 plaid fat quarters cotton fabric
    (18×22 inches)
Fat quarter green fabric (18×22 inches)
Scissors; sewing thread and needle
Metallic thread for quilting
22-inch square of batting

HERE'S HOW

1 Make templates from the patterns, *opposite*. Use the patterns to cut 9 stars from yellow fabric and the remaining shapes from plaid and green fabrics.

2 Construct nine 6-inch blocks. To green A square, add piece 1 to one side, sewing from large right angled edge of triangular piece, stopping at point marked on pattern B. Add piece 2 to A1. Sew 3 to A12. Sew piece 4 to A123. Finish sewing seam 1 to A4 side from marked point to end of block. (See top corner of diagram, *left.*)

3 Appliqué a star shape to center of each green square. Using metallic thread and buttonhole stitch, sew around star edges.

4 Cut four 1½-inch yellow squares and twelve 1½×6½-inch green strips to use as sashing. Sew sashing to blocks to complete the top.

5 Piece together scraps of plaid to make a 22-inch-square backing piece.

6 Layer top, batting, and backing fabric. Quilt as desired with metallic thread.

7 Cut 2¼-inch strips for double-fold binding edges. Sew to outside edges of quilt top. Flip to back and hand-sew the binding to the back.

Plaid Pillow Trims

shown on pages 12 and 13

WHAT YOU NEED
Scissors; ruler
Gold-glitter red felt
⅜-inch-wide satin ribbon in red,
    green, and lime green
Sewing machine; pins
Red thread; sewing needle
Pinking shears
Gold cord

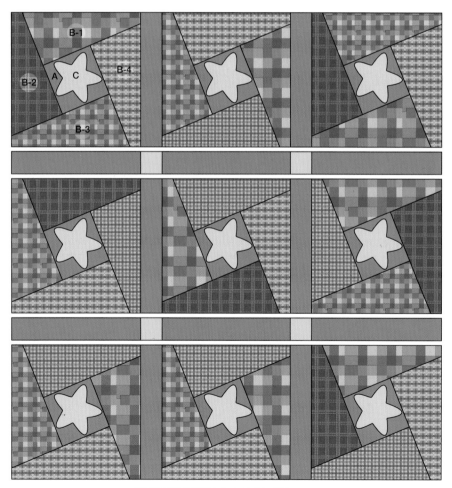

Pretty Plaid Mat Assembly Diagram

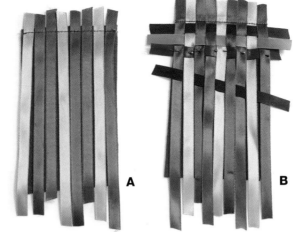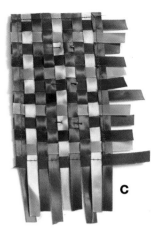

A   B   C

HERE'S HOW
to make three ornaments

Note: *The ribbons are woven in one piece, basted, and then cut apart to make three ornament fronts.*

1 Cut a piece of felt approximately 3½×11½ inches. Lay alternating ribbon colors side by side on the long length of the felt. Machine-stitch along the edge to hold the ribbons in place as shown in Step A, *above right*.

2 Cut several lengths of each ribbon color slightly longer than the short width of felt. Weave alternating ribbons as shown in Step B until length is woven, snugging the ribbons next to one another and allowing the ribbon ends to hang over the edge of the felt. After weaving about three strands, pin through all layers occasionally to keep ribbons from slipping.

3 Baste around the outside edges close to felt edges as shown in Step C. Trim the ribbons close to the felt edge.

4 Make a 2¼-inch square paper pattern. Pin the pattern on top of the completed woven piece and baste around the three squares, leaving at least ¼ inch around all sides. Cut the squares apart, leaving ¼-inch seam allowance around all edges.

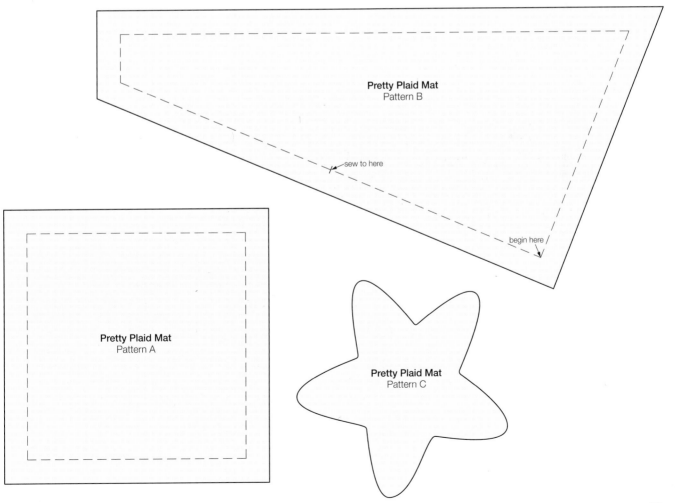

Pretty Plaid Mat
Pattern B

sew to here

begin here

Pretty Plaid Mat
Pattern A

Pretty Plaid Mat
Pattern C

On the back side of the squares, trim the felt away close to stitching, leaving ribbon edges extending ¼ inch beyond the trimmed cut edge of fabric.

5 Lay woven squares on another piece of felt and pin ribbon edges under at basting lines. Using thread to match background felt, hand-stitch square onto background felt shape, using small, invisible stitches, continuing to tuck ribbon edges under as you sew. Use pinking shears to trim background felt just beyond woven edge.

6 Stitch thin cord through top points and knot at top to hang ornaments.

Checkerboard-Cuff Stocking

shown on page 13

WHAT YOU NEED

Tracing paper; pencil
Scissors
Three 12×16-inch pieces of
    gold-glittered red felt
Ruler
⅜-inch-wide satin ribbon in red,
    green, and lime green
Red thread
Pins
Sewing needle
Pinking shears
Lime green cord
⅛-inch-wide green satin ribbon
Darning needle
Decorative brooch

HERE'S HOW

1 Enlarge and trace the stocking pattern, *opposite.* Cut out the shapes.

2 Use the patterns to cut a stocking front and back, two cuff pieces, and one star from felt.

3 Cut another piece of felt approximately 6x10 inches for the woven-ribbon cuff piece (front). Lay alternating ribbon colors side by side on the long lengths of the felt. Weave the ribbons as for ornaments on *page 19.* Baste around the outside edges close to felt edges. Trim ribbons close to felt edge.

4 Pin the cuff pattern on top of the completed square woven piece and baste around the square, leaving at least ½ inch around all sides.

5 Trim around the woven piece, leaving ½-inch seam allowance around all edges. On the back side of piece, trim the felt close to stitching, leaving ribbon edges extending ½ inch beyond the trimmed edge of fabric.

6 For the woven cuff piece, fold ribbon ends to back of felt along one long edge; machine-stitch in place. Machine-stitch the short ends to the short ends of the unwoven cuff piece.

7 Hand-tack the cording on the heal and toe sections of the stocking front. Sew the narrow green ribbon next to each piece of cording toward the center of the stocking using running stitches.

8 Make woven square for star as making ornament on *page 19.* Lay woven square on felt star shape and pin ribbon edges under at basting lines.

9 Using thread to match background felt, hand-stitch square onto background felt star, using small, invisible stitches. Tuck ribbon edges under as you sew. Use pinking shears, if desired, to trim the background felt just beyond the woven edge.

10 Sew the stocking front to the back. Sew the cuff to the stocking top. Sew on a ribbon stocking hanger. Attach the felt star to the stocking by pinning the brooch in the center.

Adirondack Stocking

shown on page 14

WHAT YOU NEED

Tracing paper; pencil
Scissors; tape measure
¼ yard of light brown shaggy plush felt
⅜ yard of red and black plaid fabric
¼ yard of red plaid fabric for binding
Assorted felt pieces in bright red, muted
    red, black, green, and tan
Matching sewing thread
Sewing machine
Large-eye needle
Homespun yarn
Size 1 embroidery needle
Cotton embroidery floss in red, gold,
    black, and green
Pewter bear button
9-inch length of cotton ribbon

HERE'S HOW

1 Trace the stocking, large circle, medium circle, and small circle patterns from *page 22* onto tracing paper; cut out the shapes.

2 From red and black plaid cut two stockings. From red plaid cut enough 2-inch-wide bias strips for 55 inches of binding. From shaggy plush felt, cut a 6×23-inch rectangle for the cuff. Referring to the photograph, *above,* for color ideas, cut nine large, nine medium, and nine small circles from felts, using the circle patterns.

3 Wrong sides together, baste the stocking front to the back using a ½-inch seam allowance, leaving the top edge open.

4 Sew together the binding strips for a continuous length. Press under ½ inch along one long edge of the binding.

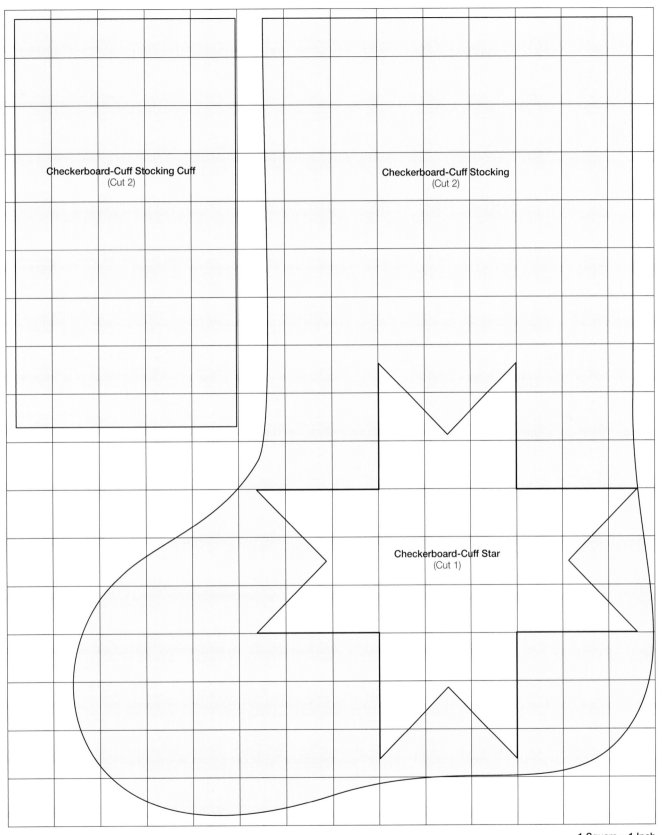

Checkerboard-Cuff Stocking Cuff
(Cut 2)

Checkerboard-Cuff Stocking
(Cut 2)

Checkerboard-Cuff Star
(Cut 1)

1 Square = 1 Inch
Enlarge at 200%

5 Right sides facing and raw edges even, place the raw edge of the binding strip on the back of the stocking. Sew the binding in place and trim the excess. Fold over the pressed edge of the binding to the stocking front, covering the stitching line. Edge-stitch the binding along the folded edge.

6 Use a large-eye needle and homespun yarn to whipstitch around binding. Weave a second length of yarn around stitches.

7 Right sides facing, sew together the narrow edges of the 6×23-inch plush felt rectangle, using a ½-inch seam allowance. Press open the seam allowance. To hem, press under ½ inch along one edge and sew ¼ inch from the fold.

8 Slip the cuff into the stocking, right side of the cuff facing the inside of the stocking, Center the cuff seam onto the stocking back seam and align raw edges. Sew the cuff to the stocking with a ½-inch seam allowance. Lay the cuff away from the stocking and press seam allowance toward the stocking. Edge-stitch around the stocking top, catching the seam allowance. Fold over the cuff.

9 Arrange the felt sets on the cuff front and whipstitch the large circles in place. Sew the bear button onto the center of one of the circles.

10 For the hanging loop thread ribbon through a large-eye needle, pull the ribbon through the fabric along the heel side of the stocking, and knot the ribbon ends together.

Adirondack Tree Skirt
shown on page 15

WHAT YOU NEED
Tracing paper; pencil; scissors
1⅜ yards of 45-inch-wide Osnaburg fabric

Yardstick
¼ yard each of two 45-inch-wide red and-black plaid fabrics
Four 9×12-inch pieces of felt in shades of green
⅝ yard of Sherpa fabric; straight pins
Black cotton embroidery floss
Size 3 embroidery needle
Matching sewing thread
Fabric marking pen

HERE'S HOW
1 Trace and cut out the tree pattern, *opposite*, onto tracing paper. From the Osnaburg, cut a 32-inch square for the back. Cut thirteen 6¾-inch squares. From each of the red and black plaid fabrics, cut six 6¾-inch squares. From the felt cut a total of seven trees. From the Sherpa fabric tear or cut binding strips from selvage to selvage, tearing one 2-inch-wide strip for the center back opening and three 4¾-inch-wide strips for the skirt edges.

2 Position and pin each tree onto an Osnaburg square, centering four trees diagonally on the skirt corner squares and centering three trees straight on the squares for the skirt sides. Use the embroidery needle and three plies of black floss to whipstitch the trees to the squares.

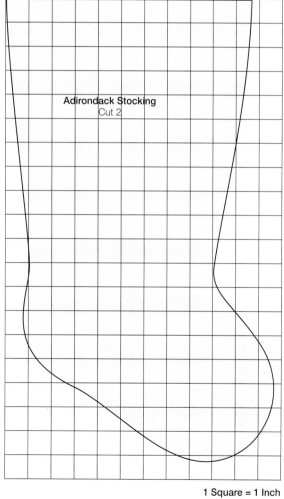

Adirondack Stocking
Cut 2

1 Square = 1 Inch
Enlarge at 400%

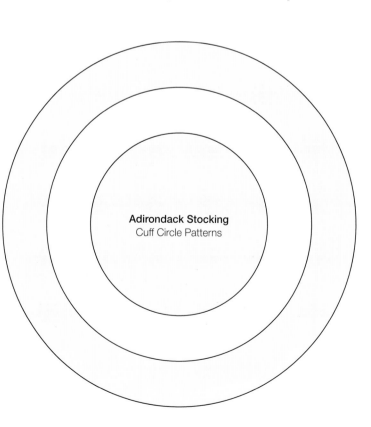

Adirondack Stocking
Cuff Circle Patterns

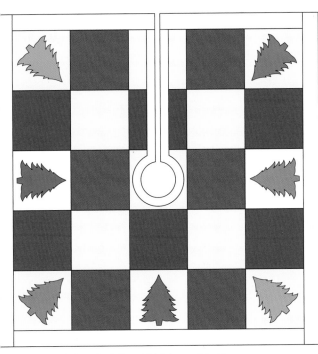

Adirondack Tree Skirt Assembly Diagram

Adirondack Tree Skirt
Tree Pattern

3 Referring to the Assembly Diagram, *above*, lay out the squares on a flat surface. Sew the squares together in rows using a ¼-inch seam allowance; press the seam allowances toward the plaid squares. Sew the rows together; press the seam allowances in the same direction.

4 Smooth out the skirt back on a flat surface. Place the pieced skirt front faceup on the back. Pin the layers together. For the skirt opening, use a fabric marking pen

to draw a 5⅛-inch-diameter circle on the skirt front, centering the circle on the center Osnaburg square. For the center back opening, use yardstick and a fabric marking pen to draw a line from the tree skirt center to the outer edge. Pin along the drawn lines. Using a ¼-inch seam allowance, baste the outer edges of the front and back together. Sew ¼ inch from the circle and along both sides of the drawn line. Carefully cut through both layers on the lines.

5 To bind the center back opening, align the raw edges and pin the 2-inch-wide Sherpa strip around the opening on the back of the tree skirt. Sew the strip to the skirt using a ¼-inch seam allowance. Trim any excess fabric from the ends of the binding strip. Press the seam allowances toward the binding. Fold the binding over to the front of the tree skirt, overlapping the stitching line by ¼ inch. Topstitch the binding in place through all layers a scant ¼ inch from the torn edge. Bind the outer edges of the tree skirt in the same manner, using the 4¾-inch-wide strips and piecing the strips as needed.

christmas paper fun

Choose colors of your favorite papers that reflect the season and let them inspire you to have some paper fun.

For a simple yet stunning look for your
Christmas tree this year, make a **Holiday Hue
Garland**, *opposite*, from small pieces of paper
and sparkling beads. The pieces don't have
to all be the same—let the kids help make this
fun addition to your tree. Using only round
paper shapes, this **Paper Tree Trio**, *above*,
says Merry Christmas with three times the
heart. Instructions for these paper projects
are on *page 36*.

Make everyone on your Christmas card list smile when they open cards you have created yourself. The **Holiday Poinsettia Card**, *opposite*, has a lovely 3-D paper construction. The jolly old elf's suit is inspiration for **Well-Suited Greetings**, *right*. Create **A Joyful Gesture**, *above*, using pretty Christmas-color scrapbook papers. Instructions and patterns are on *pages 36–37*.

Happy Ho...appy
...cake frui...
...joy joy joy joy j...
magic magic magic magic
snow snow   snow s...
hot cocoa hot   cocoa hot c...
Santa Santa   Santa Santa
Rudolph Rudolp   Rudolph Rudolp
family family   family family
mittens mittens   mittens mittens
stockings Stock   stockings Stock
gingerbread gingerbread gingerbread gin
ery Merry Merry Merry Merry Merry M
as Christmas Christmas Christmas C
ve love love love love love, love, love,
ameron Cameron Cameron Cameron Cam
l 2006 2006 2006 2006 2006 2006 2006 2006 20
peace peace peace peace peace peace peace

let it snow
let it snow !
let it snow !

Merry Christmas 2006

Share **Surprising Tidings**, *opposite*, with friends and family

by making your own set of winter cards. Dress up a tree,

frame a photo, or build a paper snowman to hang on a tree

or doorknob. **Fanciful Frames**, *above*, are easy to make using

purchased "to and from" stickers or cards in your favorite

colors and styles. Frame a photo or a favorite greeting card.

Instructions for the projects are on *pages 38–39*.

Add **Finishing Touches** to your gifts by making personal gift tags that are sure to bring smiles. Make the tags using bits and pieces of scrapbooking papers, ribbons, stickers, and other clever finds. Instructions are on *pages 39–41*.

JeanAnne

to: Ellen
Merry Christmas & Beth

to: Jonathon
from: Santa Claus

Elliot

Use favorite holiday motifs to create cards and gift bags.

A simple tree shape is just the beginning for a 3-D

Tree Punch Card, *above*. Stars, trees, and holly leaves

make gift bags that are **Star Attractions**, *opposite*. Make

them in no time using purchased gift bags and snippets

of paper and ribbon. Instructions for all of the projects

are on *pages 41–43*.

Give them something to take home that they will treasure. Make **Festive Favors** using favorite family recipes written on recipe cards tucked into colorful library card envelopes. Display them as centerpieces or add them to each place setting. Instructions are on *page 42*.

Holiday Hue Garland

shown on page 24

WHAT YOU NEED

Lime green card stock
Vellum in red and lime green
Pinking shears
Needle
Dental floss
Clear tri beads

HERE'S HOW

1 Cut several 1×1⅝-inch rectangles from card stock and vellum using pinking shears. Use the needle to poke a hole in the center of each paper rectangle.

2 Cut a length of dental floss the desired length of garland. Tie a tri bead onto one end. Thread on five more beads. To make the garland pattern, thread on a red vellum rectangle, three beads, a green card stock rectangle, three beads, a green vellum rectangle, three beads, a green card stock rectangle, and three beads. Repeat from beginning of garland pattern until the desired length is achieved. Thread on six beads, knotting the last bead on the floss to secure.

Paper Tree Trio

shown on page 25

WHAT YOU NEED

Newspapers
¾-inch wood spools
Acrylic paint in red, white, and silver
Paintbrush; circle cutter
6-inch wood snowflake
Assorted solid and print green
   card stock
Cutting mat; crafts knife
³⁄₁₆-inch wood dowels
Hot-glue gun and glue sticks
Silver miniature star tree topper

HERE'S HOW

1 Cover the work surface with newspapers. Determine the desired height of the tree and how many spools will be needed. Paint half of the spools white and the remaining spools red. Paint the snowflake silver. Let the paint dry.

2 Using the circle cutter, cut several circles from card stock, varying the sizes from approximately 1 inch to 6 inches in diameter. On a cutting mat cut an X in the center of each circle using a crafts knife.

3 Cut the dowel to the desired height, allowing room for the star topper.

4 Glue a spool in the center of the snowflake. Put a small amount of hot glue on one end of the dowel and push into the spool, holding firmly until set. Thread spools onto the dowel, alternating colors and adding paper circles when desired. Glue the star topper to the tip of the dowel.

Holiday Poinsettia Card

shown on page 26

WHAT YOU NEED

Tracing paper
Pencil; scissors
Mulberry paper in yellow, bright pink,
   red, burgundy, and lime green
Glue stick
Toothpicks; ruler
11×5-inch pieces of white card stock
6-inch-square envelopes

HERE'S HOW

1 Trace the poinsettia patterns, *right*. Cut out the shapes. Use the patterns to

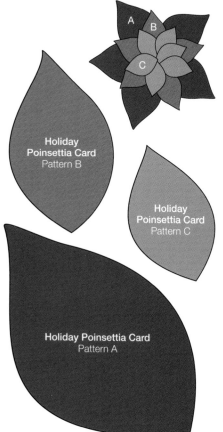

cut 10 large burgundy petals, 10 medium red petals, and 12 small pink petals.

2 To make a vein in each petal, rub glue stick on one side of a petal. Lay a toothpick on the glue in the center of the petal; press a second petal atop the first. Cut off any toothpick that extends beyond the paper.

3 Fold the card stock in half, short ends together. Cut a 5-inch square from yellow mulberry paper and adhere it in the center of the card front. Cut a 4⅜-inch square from green paper; adhere it in the center of the yellow paper.

4 Starting with the large petals, glue all of the poinsettia petals to the card front. Cut a 1-inch square from yellow paper; crinkle and glue to flower center.

Holiday Poinsettia Card
Pattern B

Holiday Poinsettia Card
Pattern C

Holiday Poinsettia Card
Pattern A

Well-Suited Greetings

shown on page 27

WHAT YOU NEED

Tracing paper; pencil
Scissors
Red card stock
11½×5¾-inch piece of card
    stock in purple or turquoise
Glue stick
5-inch square of paper in green
    plaid or metallic gold
4½-inch square of white card stock
Chenille stems in white, black, and
    silver or gold
Hot-glue gun and glue sticks
6-inch-square envelopes

HERE'S HOW

1 Trace the pattern, *above right.* Cut out the shape. Use the pattern to cut a coat shape from red card stock.
2 Fold the rectangular piece of card stock in half, short ends together. Use glue stick to adhere the background papers to the center of the card front. Glue the red coat shape to the card front.
3 Holding the center of a white chenille stem at the middle of the coat collar area, shape the chenille stem to make a collar and to detail the front and bottom edges of the coat.
4 Cut a short piece of chenille stem to trim each cuff. Hot-glue the chenille stem pieces to the coat. Add a black chenille stem belt and a rectangular buckle made from a short piece cut from silver or gold chenille stem.

Well-Suited Greetings Coat Pattern

Well-Suited
Greetings
Placement
Diagram

A Joyful Gesture

shown on page 27

WHAT YOU NEED

Tracing paper; pencil; scissors
Mulberry paper in lime green and
    dark green
9×8-inch piece of pink card stock
6⅝×3-inch piece of white card stock
7⅛×3⅛-inch piece of bright pink
    mulberry paper
7½×3⅝-inch piece of pink and green
    striped paper
Glue stick
Five ⅜-inch lime green mosaic
    sticker tiles
Toothpicks
Scraps of bright pink mulberry paper
Alphabet stickers
Coordinating business envelopes

HERE'S HOW

1 Trace the patterns, *page 38*; cut out shapes. Use the patterns to cut two holly pairs from lime green and one pair from dark green as shown in diagram, *right.*
2 Fold the pink card stock in half, 9-inch ends together. Use glue stick to adhere the white card stock in the center of the bright pink mulberry paper; adhere to center of stripe paper. Adhere the paper layers to the card front, ¼ inch from the right-hand edge. Press five sticker tiles equally spaced ⅛ inch from the edge of the stripe paper.

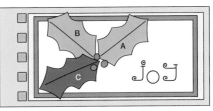

3 To make a vein in each holly leaf, rub glue stick onto one side of a leaf. Lay a toothpick on the glue in the center of the leaf; press a second leaf atop the first. Cut off any toothpick that extends beyond the paper. Make a toothpick vein for each leaf.
4 Using the photo as a guide, glue the three holly leaves to the card front. Cut three 1-inch squares from pink mulberry paper. Roll each square into a ball to look like a berry. Glue the berries in the center of the holly arrangement.
5 Use sticker letters to spell "joy" in the lower right corner of the card.

A Joyful Gesture Placement Diagram

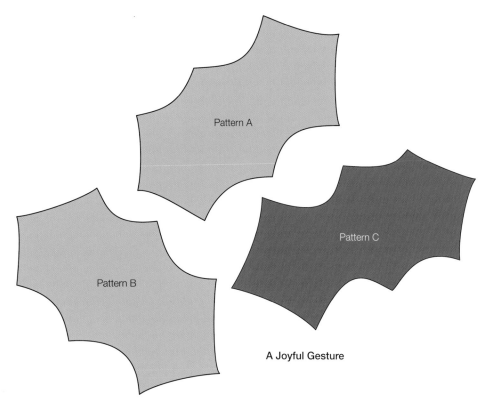

Pattern A

Pattern C

Pattern B

A Joyful Gesture

Surprising Tidings
shown on page 28

WHAT YOU NEED
for the tree-trimming card
8½×11-inch white paper
Pencil; scissors
8½×11-inch dark blue card stock
Silver gel pen
Small hole punch
5×7-inch or smaller silver paper
Crafts glue
Silver leaf skeleton
Silver cord
Silver star sequin
Red sequins

HERE'S HOW
1 Draw a 9-inch-tall star-topped tree shape onto white paper, using the photo, *right*, as a reference. Cut out the shape. Use the pattern to trace the tree onto blue card stock; cut out.
2 Use silver pen to write "Merry Christmas 2006" along the bottom of the blue tree front. If desired, write a personal message on the back with the pen. Punch a hole in the center of the star.
3 Draw a star on the silver paper, sizing it to fit within the tree's blue star. Cut out the star and punch a hole in the center.

Glue the silver star onto the star at the top of the tree, aligning the holes. From the leaf skeleton cut a tree shape, using the stem of the leaf as the trunk. Glue the leaf tree onto the card front using tiny dots of crafts glue.
4 For the hanging loop, thread silver cord through the holes. If desired (as shown on *page 28*), slip a star sequin onto an end of the cord before knotting the ends and tying the bow. Randomly glue red sequins onto the leaf tree.

WHAT YOU NEED
for the Magnetic Attraction Card
5×7-inch precut mat with a
    1½×2½-inch photo opening
7×9-inch rectangle of dark green paper
Crafts knife
Clear tape
Gold gel pen
Photograph to fit 1½×2½-inch opening
4½×6½-inch rectangle of dark green
    art paper
Crafts glue
Two 4-inch pieces of ½-inch-wide
    adhesive magnetic strip
18-inch piece of 1½-inch-wide
    wire-edge plaid ribbon

HERE'S HOW
1 Center the precut mat facedown on 7×9-inch dark green paper. Fold the paper around the outer edges of the mat to the back, trimming at the corners to reduce bulk; secure with tape. Use a crafts knife to cut the paper inside the opening from corner to corner, making an X to create four triangular flaps. Fold flaps to the back covering edges of opening; tape to secure.
2 Use gold gel pen to write a greeting below the opening. Center and tape the photo in the opening. Glue the remaining piece of art paper to the back. Remove the paper backing from the magnetic strips. Press strips vertically onto the card back to the left and right of the photo opening.
3 Trace over the greeting with the gel pen so that it stands out. Fill the card with more greetings.
4 Make a bow with the ribbon. Glue the bow to the top of the card.

WHAT YOU NEED
for the Welcoming Ways Card

Scissors; pencil; crafts knife

³⁄₃₂×4×9-inch piece of balsa wood or
    mat board

Acrylic paints in light pearl blue, blue,
    white, green, black, and orange

Assorted paintbrushes; toothpicks

Fine-tip silver paint pen

4×6¼-inch blue paper, optional

Crafts glue

Medium-tip silver paint pen

Fine white glitter

Marking pens in red and green

½×8-inch strip of white fleece

Two ³⁄₈-inch diameter black buttons

Two 1½-inch lengths of twigs

HERE'S HOW

1 Use a photocopy machine to enlarge
the snowman pattern, *right*, approximately
250 percent so that snowman with hat
measures approximately 7 inches tall; cut
out snowman and hat. Center cut pattern
on the 4×9-inch piece of balsa or mat
board; trace with a pencil.

2 Use the crafts knife to cut out the hat.
Go over the hat outline several times with
the crafts knife before cutting through the
balsa or mat board. Work slowly and be
careful not to break the wood. Check to
be sure the hat opening is large enough to
hang on a door handle.

3 With a pencil lightly draw a face,
scarf, buttons, and arms. Mix light pearl

Snowman Pattern

let it snow
let it snow
let it snow

blue paint with blue paint; paint the
background. Paint the snowman white
and shade with the mixed light blue. Paint
the buttons, arms, mouth, and eyes in
black, using the tip of a toothpick to make
the dots. Paint the carrot nose orange. Use
white paint to dot snowflakes on the
background. Let the paint dry. Use green
and red marking pens to stripe the fleece
for the scarf.

4 Use the fine-tip silver paint pen to write
"let it snow" or another holiday phrase
below the snowman. If desired, write a
longer personal message on the blue paper
and glue it to the back of the door hanger.

5 Use the fine- and medium-tip silver
paint pens to add details and to outline
the snowman. Use toothpicks to add drops
of glue to the white snowflakes. Sprinkle
glitter over the glue; gently shake off
excess glitter. Let dry.

6 Use the crafts knife to make slits through
the wood or mat board on each side of the
snowman's neck. Insert the ends of the
scarf through the slits from the back to the
front; knot the scarf under the snowman's
chin. Glue on buttons and twig arms.

Fanciful Frames
shown on page 29

WHAT YOU NEED

Flat white picture frame

Assorted sticker gift tags

Decoupage medium, optional

Holiday art to fit in frame, such
    as a greeting card, scrapbook
    embellishment, or child's drawing

Scissors

Card stock, optional

HERE'S HOW

1 Apply the sticker gift tags randomly on
the front of the frame, wrapping tags to
the frame back when necessary. Coat the
frame with decoupage medium if desired.
2 Place the art in the frame, trimming to
fit or backing with card stock if needed.

Finishing Touches
shown on pages 30–31

WHAT YOU NEED
for the sticker tags

Blue card stock; scissors

Stickers, such as framed oval, name
    tag, snowman, or lace heart

Decorative-edge scissors, optional

Fine-tip blue or black marking pen, or
    silver gel pen

¼-inch silver metal grommet and
    hammer, optional; hole punch

12- to 15-inch piece of ½-inch-wide
    sheer ribbon, ³⁄₈-inch-wide trim, fine
    string, or metal ball chain

christmas paper fun

HERE'S HOW

1 Apply a sticker to card stock. Trim the paper, creating an even border on all edges or allowing writing space along one edge. If desired, use decorative-edge scissors to cut the paper.

2 Use marker or pen to write a greeting and the gift recipient's name on the tag.

3 Use a small hole punch to make a hole in the top of the tag or apply a grommet following the manufacturer's instructions. Thread ribbon, trim, string, or ball chain through the hole, and attach tag to package.

WHAT YOU NEED
for the sand dollar tag
Fine-tip blue marking pen
Sand dollar
15-inch piece of ⅜-inch-wide
    blue sheer ribbon

HERE'S HOW

1 Use a marking pen to write a greeting and "To" and "From" on the front of the sand dollar.

2 Thread ribbon through one opening on the sand dollar and tie tag to package.

WHAT YOU NEED
for the fleur-de-lis tag
Precut silver fleur-de-lis (available at
    crafts stores)
Crafts glue
2¼×3¼-inch piece of blue card stock
2¾×3¾-inch piece of silver art paper
Silver gel pen
Hole punch; 8-inch piece of silver cord

HERE'S HOW

1 Glue the fleur-de-lis onto the blue rectangle, then glue the blue rectangle onto silver rectangle.

2 Use the silver pen to write the gift recipient's name below the fleur-de-lis.

3 Use a small hole punch to make a hole at the top left corner of the tag. Thread silver cord through the hole and tie the tag to the package.

WHAT YOU NEED
for the foam star tag
Tracing paper; pencil
Cookie cutter, optional
Blue crafts foam
Permanent black marking pen

¼-inch silver metal grommet and
    hammer; scissors
16-inch piece of ¾-inch-wide
    check ribbon

HERE'S HOW

1 With a pencil draw a star shape onto tracing paper, drawing freehand or using a cookie cutter; cut out. Trace star onto foam; cut out.

2 Use a marking pen to write the gift recipient's name centered on the star.

3 Apply a grommet at the center top of the star, following the manufacturer's instructions. Thread ribbon through the grommet and tie the tag to the package.

WHAT YOU NEED
for the silver swirl tag
2×3-inch piece of decorative silver
    paper with white swirls; scissors
Hole punch
1⅜×2-inch piece of white card stock
Fine-tip silver marking pen; crafts glue
14-inch piece of white satin cord

HERE'S HOW

1 Trim off the corners on one short edge of decorative paper. Punch a hole between the trimmed corners.

2 Use a silver marking pen to write the gift recipient's name centered on the white rectangle. Glue the white rectangle onto the decorative paper. Thread satin cord through the hole and tie the tag to the package.

WHAT YOU NEED
for the embossed tags
Office supply tag or
    2-inch-diameter circle
    for patterns

Pencil; scissors
Dark blue card stock; silver gel pen
Pinking shears, optional
Rubber stamp in reindeer or
    ornament motif
Embossing gel pad and pen
Embossing powder in silver and red
Heat source, such as an embossing
    heat tool, toaster, or clothes iron
Small paintbrush; hole punch
12-inch piece of narrow silver cord or
    elastic cord
Two small silver jingle bells, optional

HERE'S HOW

1 For the reindeer tag use a pencil to trace the office supply tag onto card stock; cut out. For the ornament tag use silver pen to trace the 2-inch-diameter circle onto card stock, using pinking shears to cut out ¼ inch beyond circle.

2 For either tag, ink the stamp with embossing gel and stamp the image onto the tag. Immediately sprinkle silver embossing powder on the image. Tilt the tag on edge and tap off the excess powder. Use the heat tool to melt the powder according to the manufacturer's directions, creating a shiny, raised image. Use the embossing gel pen to make a circle for the reindeer's nose. Sprinkle the nose with red embossing powder. Tap off excess powder and carefully remove any stray powder with a paintbrush. Emboss the nose with the heat tool.

3 Use a small hole punch to make a hole at the center top of the tag. Use the silver pen to write the gift recipient's name on the tag. Thread silver cord through the hole and tie the tag to the package. If desired, tie jingle bells to the ends of the cord.

WHAT YOU NEED
for the snowflake tag
Light blue marking pen
Metal-edge circle tag
Crafts glue; toothpicks; glitter
Hole punch
Fine-tip black marking pen
14-inch piece of light blue chenille cord

HERE'S HOW
1 Use light blue marking pen to draw a snowflake freehand on the center of the metal-edge circle tag. Use a toothpick to apply crafts glue over the lines of the snowflake. Immediately sprinkle glitter on the glue; let glue dry.

2 Use a small hole punch to make a hole at the center top of the tag. Use black marking pen to write the gift recipient's name on the tag. Thread cord through the hole and tie the tag to the package.

Tree Punch Card
shown on page 33 and above for options

WHAT YOU NEED
Variety of scrapbook papers, including green paper for the tree; scissors
Ruler
Glue stick
$4\frac{5}{8} \times 6\frac{1}{4}$-inch blank card with envelope

Tracing paper; pencil
Scallop-edge scissors
Assorted paper punches, such as stars, circles, and bows
Fine silver cording
Star sequin

HERE'S HOW
1 From the scrapbook papers cut as many rectangles as you'd like for the front of the card. The large rectangle is $4\frac{1}{8} \times 5\frac{3}{4}$ inches, and the small one is $3\frac{3}{8} \times 5$ inches. Center the rectangles on the front of the card and glue them in place.

2 Use a pencil to trace the tree pattern, *right*, onto tracing paper. Cut out the pattern. Draw around the tree shape on green scrapbook paper and cut it out.

3 For the pieced tree use the scallop-edge scissors to cut the tree shape into sections, referring to the photo, *above right*. Punch shapes in the tree sections for decorations. Also punch shapes from paper scraps for more decorations, including a star for the treetop. Glue them to the tree.

4 For a layered tree use paper punches to make decorative shapes. Use glue stick to mount the tree onto a piece of contrasting paper. Be sure to select a paper that will show through the punched shapes. Trim away the excess paper from the edges of the tree.

5 To make the tree removable to use as an ornament, position it on the card front. Using a small circle hole punch, make two holes near the treetop through all layers. Cut a 6-inch length of fine silver cording. Working from the inside of the card, thread the cording ends through the card, the tree, and a sequin. Knot the cording ends together and trim off the excess. Or simply mount the layered tree onto the front of the card using the glue stick.

Tree Punch Cards
Pattern

patterns to cut additional shapes. To layer the shapes, cut two of the same shape and trim the edges of one to make it smaller. Glue the layers together onto the front of the bag.

9 Punch a hole through the tag with the circle hole punch. Attach the tag to the bag handle with string. Wrap a gift with tissue paper and place it in the bag.

Festive Favors

shown on pages 34–35

WHAT YOU NEED

Library card envelopes (available where teaching supplies are sold)
Alphabet stickers
Scrapbooking embellishments
Recipe cards containing favorite holiday recipes
Pedestal bowl filled with holiday shred and ornaments

HERE'S HOW

1 Using alphabet stickers, adhere a holiday word on the front of the library card envelope.

2 Trim around the word with scrapbooking embellishments.

3 Slip a recipe card into the envelope. Tuck several envelopes into the decorated pedestal bowl.

Star Attractions

shown on page 32

WHAT YOU NEED

Solid-color paper gift bag and tissue paper
Tape measure
Assorted ribbons
Scissors
Crafts glue
Double-sided tape
Pencil
Tracing paper
Patterned scrapbook papers
Assorted buttons, including
⅝-inch-diameter red buttons for the holly berries
Paper punches in star and ¼-inch circle shapes
Card stock in yellow and white
White string

HERE'S HOW

1 Open the paper gift bag. Use a tape measure to find the distance around the opened bag. Add ½ inch to this number and use it to measure and cut lengths of ribbon. Use one color of ribbon or layer several colors.

2 Apply crafts glue or double-sided tape to the back of the widest ribbon. Wrap the ribbon around the bag, overlapping the ends at the back of the bag. Glue or tape any additional ribbons centered on the wide ribbon.

3 Depending on the size of the bag, select the pattern, *opposite*, for the tree, star, or holly design. Trace the patterns needed onto tracing paper and cut them out.

4 Draw around the patterns onto the wrong side of the patterned scrapbook paper. Cut out the shapes and glue them to the bag front.

5 Glue on buttons for tree decorations or holly berries. Add buttons to the ribbon trim if desired.

6 To add stars to the bag handle, use the paper punch to make stars from the yellow card stock. Glue them to the front of the handle.

7 To make a gift tag, fold the piece of white card stock in half. Many shapes will work as long as the folded edge is kept as part of the card shape. For the star tag trace the large star pattern with one star point on the fold.

8 Decorate the tag as desired, referring to the photos, *above*, for ideas. Use the

Star Attractions
Tree, Holly, and Star
Patterns

cookies galore

Christmastime is cookie time, so create an array of treats to delight everyone—from a kid-pleasing chocolate and peanut butter combo to sophisticated meringues.

Lavish **Peppermint-Stick Spritz,** *opposite,* with white chocolate and crushed peppermint candies for unforgettable results. With a citrus-curd filling nestled between nut-infused disks, **Almond-Lime Macaroons,** *above,* might just be the most elegant cookie on this year's tray. Recipes are on *page 52.*

Peanut butter works its nutty magic in two very different cookies.
Choose **PB&C Cookie Sandwiches,** *above left,* when you want
a big, sweet cookie kids will love. **Peanut Butter Macaroons,**
above center, are the choice to show off a more sophisticated side
of peanut butter. The magic ingredient in **Chocolate Chip**
Thumbprints, *opposite,* is the luscious chocolate-hazelnut spread.
Recipes are on *pages 52–53.*

Pistachio Shortbread, *above,* is the ticket when you want a rich, buttery cookie to go with coffee or tea. Everyone appreciates a light, airy cookie to balance the richer delights on a cookie tray. **Hazelnut Meringues**, *opposite top,* will do nicely! Give **Chocolate-Raisin and Oatmeal Cookie Mix**, *opposite,* and recipients can bake the treats at their leisure. Recipes are on *pages 54–55.*

With **Cherry-Almond Cutouts**, *opposite,*
you can enjoy all the whimsy of a cutout cookie
with a fruit-and-nut angle to make it special.
Sables, *above,* are tender, melt-in-your-mouth
butter cookies with an unmistakably Christmas
touch. Recipes are on *page 55.*

Peppermint-Stick Spritz

shown on page 44

WHAT YOU NEED

- ¾ cup butter, softened
- ½ cup sugar
- 1 teaspoon baking powder
- 1 egg
- ½ teaspoon peppermint extract or 7 drops peppermint oil
- 1¾ cups all-purpose flour
- 6 ounces white baking chocolate, chopped
- 1 tablespoon shortening
- ⅓ cup finely crushed striped round peppermint candies

HERE'S HOW

1 Preheat oven to 375°F. In a large mixing bowl beat butter with an electric mixer on medium to high speed for 30 seconds. Beat in sugar and baking powder until combined, scraping sides of bowl occasionally. Beat in egg and peppermint extract or oil until combined. Beat in as much of the flour as you can with the mixer. Stir in any remaining flour.

2 Pack unchilled dough into a cookie press fitted with a ½-inch star plate. Force dough through press to form 3½- to 4-inch-long sticks about 1 inch apart on an ungreased cookie sheet. If desired, bend into candy-cane shapes.

3 Bake for 7 to 9 minutes or until edges are firm but not brown. Transfer cookies to wire racks and let cool.

4 In a small heavy saucepan melt white chocolate and shortening over low heat, stirring frequently. Dip one end of each stick into melted white chocolate, letting excess drip off. Place on waxed paper. Sprinkle with crushed peppermint candy. Let stand until set. Makes about 60 cookies.

To store: Place cookies in layers separated by waxed paper in an airtight container; cover. Store at room temperature for up to 3 days. Or place undipped cookies in a freezer container; cover and freeze for up to 3 months. Thaw cookies; dip them in melted white chocolate and sprinkle with crushed peppermint candy.

Almond-Lime Macaroons

shown on page 45

WHAT YOU NEED

- 2 egg whites
- 1 tablespoon amaretto or ¼ teaspoon almond extract
- ½ teaspoon vanilla
- ¼ teaspoon cream of tartar
- ½ cup sugar
- 2 tablespoons all-purpose flour
- 1½ cups ground almonds
- 1 3-ounce package cream cheese, softened
- ¼ cup lime curd or lemon curd

HERE'S HOW

1 In a medium mixing bowl let egg whites stand at room temperature for 30 minutes. Meanwhile, line two cookie sheets with parchment paper or foil; set aside.

2 Preheat oven to 300°F. Add the amaretto, vanilla, and cream of tartar to the egg whites. Beat with an electric mixer on medium speed until soft peaks form (tips curl). Gradually add sugar, 1 tablespoon at a time, beating on high speed until stiff peaks form (tips stand straight). Beat in flour just until combined. Gently fold in almonds.

3 Spoon mixture into a decorating bag fitted with a ½-inch round tip. Pipe 1-inch mounds 1½ inches apart onto the prepared cookie sheets. (Or place the mixture in a resealable plastic bag, snip off one of the corners, and pipe as above. Or drop mixture from a teaspoon to make 1-inch cookies.)

4 Bake both cookie sheets on separate oven racks for 10 minutes or until cookies are set. Turn off oven and let cookies dry in oven with the door closed for 30 minutes. Transfer cookies to wire racks and let cool completely.

5 Up to 2 hours before serving, in a medium mixing bowl, beat cream cheese with an electric mixer on medium speed for 30 seconds. Beat in lime curd until smooth. Spread on flat sides of half of the macaroons; top with remaining macaroons. Cover and chill until served. Makes about 20 sandwich cookies.

To store: Place unfilled cookies in layers separated by waxed paper in an airtight container; cover. Store at room temperature for up to 1 week; fill before serving. Or place unfilled cookies in a freezer container; cover and freeze for up to 3 months. Thaw cookies and fill before serving.

PB&C Cookie Sandwiches

shown on page 46

WHAT YOU NEED

- ½ cup butter, softened
- ½ cup granulated sugar
- ½ cup packed brown sugar

½ teaspoon baking soda
½ teaspoon salt
1 egg
1 teaspoon vanilla
1 cup all-purpose flour
½ cup unsweetened cocoa powder
1 11-ounce package peanut butter and milk chocolate pieces
½ cup purchased chocolate frosting
½ cup peanut butter

HERE'S HOW

1 In a large mixing bowl beat butter with an electric mixer on medium to high speed for 30 seconds. Add granulated sugar, brown sugar, baking soda, and salt. Beat until combined. Add egg and vanilla. Beat until combined. Beat in as much of the flour as you can with the mixer. Stir in any remaining flour and the cocoa powder. Stir in peanut butter and milk chocolate pieces. Cover and chill dough for 2 to 3 hours or until easy to handle.

2 Preheat oven to 375°F. Lightly grease cookie sheets. Roll dough into 1-inch balls. Place 2 inches apart on prepared cookie sheets. Flatten cookies slightly with a glass dipped in sugar to about ⅜ inch thick. Bake for 7 to 8 minutes or until tops are cracked and look dry. Let cool on cookie sheets for 1 minute. Transfer cookies to wire racks and let cool completely.

3 In a small bowl stir together frosting and peanut butter. Spread a scant 2 teaspoons frosting mixture on the bottoms of half of the cookies. Top with remaining cookies, bottom sides together. Makes 24 sandwich cookies.

To store: Place sandwich cookies in layers separated by waxed paper in an airtight container; cover. Store at room temperature for up to 24 hours. Or place cookies in a freezer container; cover and freeze for up to 3 months.

Peanut Butter Macaroons

shown on page 46

WHAT YOU NEED

2 egg whites
⅛ teaspoon cream of tartar
Dash salt
½ cup sugar
½ cup creamy peanut butter
2 cups chocolate-flavored crisp rice cereal
⅓ cup chopped honey-roasted peanuts
1 cup semisweet chocolate pieces, optional
2 teaspoons shortening, optional
Chopped honey-roasted peanuts, optional

HERE'S HOW

1 Preheat oven to 300°F. Lightly grease two cookie sheets or line with parchment paper; set aside.

2 In a medium mixing bowl beat egg whites, cream of tartar, and salt with an electric mixer on high speed until soft peaks form (tips curl). Gradually add sugar, 1 tablespoon at a time, beating until stiff peaks form (tips stand straight). Gently fold in peanut butter. Fold in cereal. Drop mixture by rounded teaspoons 2 inches apart onto the prepared cookie sheets. Sprinkle with chopped peanuts.

3 Bake for 10 minutes. Turn off oven and let cookies dry in oven with the door closed for 15 minutes. Remove macaroons from cookie sheets to wire racks and let cool completely.

4 If desired, in a small saucepan melt chocolate pieces and shortening over low heat. Place chocolate in a small resealable plastic bag. Seal bag and snip off a tiny corner. Drizzle macaroons with chocolate and sprinkle with a few additional peanuts. Makes about 30 cookies.

Chocolate Chip Thumbprints

shown on page 47

WHAT YOU NEED

1 18-ounce roll refrigerated chocolate-chip cookie dough
⅓ cup all-purpose flour
¾ cup finely chopped hazelnuts (filberts) or almonds
¼ cup milk
½ cup purchased chocolate-hazelnut spread
Candy sprinkles

HERE'S HOW

1 Preheat oven to 375°F. In a large mixing bowl knead together the cookie dough and flour until combined. Shape tablespoon-size pieces of dough into balls. Place nuts in a shallow dish. Place milk in another shallow dish. Roll dough balls in milk and then in nuts. Place balls 2 inches apart on an ungreased cookie sheet. Press your thumb into the center of each ball to make an indentation.

2 Bake for 10 to 12 minutes or until lightly browned. Transfer cookies to a wire rack and let cool. Place chocolate-hazelnut spread in a resealable plastic bag; snip off one of the corners. Pipe spread into each indentation. Sprinkle cookies with candy sprinkles. Makes about 30 cookies.

To store: Place unfilled cookies in layers separated by waxed paper in an airtight container; cover. Store in the refrigerator for up to 3 days; fill and decorate before serving. Or place unfilled cookies in a freezer container; cover and freeze for up to 3 months. Thaw cookies, fill, and decorate before serving.

Pistachio Shortbread

shown on page 48

WHAT YOU NEED

1¾ cups all-purpose flour
  1 cup finely ground pistachio nuts
  ⅓ cup sugar
  1 cup butter
1½ cups white baking pieces
  1 tablespoon shortening
  1 cup finely chopped pistachio nuts

HERE'S HOW

1 Preheat oven to 325°F. In a medium bowl combine flour, ground pistachio nuts, and sugar. Using a pastry blender, cut in butter until mixture resembles fine crumbs and starts to cling together. Form mixture into a ball; knead until smooth. Divide dough in half.

2 On a lightly floured surface, roll one portion of the dough into an 8×4-inch rectangle. Using a fluted vegetable cutter (crinkle cutter) or fluted pastry wheel, cut dough into 2×¾-inch rectangles and/or 1-inch squares. Place about 2 inches apart on ungreased cookie sheets. Repeat with remaining dough.

3 Bake for 15 to 18 minutes or until edges are firm and bottoms are very lightly browned. Transfer cookies to wire racks and let cool.

4 Line cookie sheets with waxed paper; set aside. In a small saucepan cook and stir white baking pieces and shortening over low heat until smooth. Dip one end or corner of each cookie into melted mixture. Place dipped cookies on prepared cookie sheets. Sprinkle dipped portion with some of the chopped pistachio nuts. Chill about 15 minutes or until coating is set. Makes 24 to 30 cookies.

To store: Place cookies in layers separated by waxed paper in an airtight container; cover. Store in a cool, dry place for up to 3 days. Or place cookies in a freezer container; cover and freeze for up to 1 month.

Hazelnut Meringues

shown on page 49

WHAT YOU NEED

  2 egg whites
  ½ teaspoon vanilla
  ¼ teaspoon cream of tartar
  ⅔ cup sugar
  2 teaspoons hazelnut liqueur, crème de cacao, or your favorite liqueur
     Whole hazelnuts (filberts)
  ½ cup milk chocolate pieces
  2 teaspoons shortening

HERE'S HOW

1 In a large mixing bowl let egg whites stand at room temperature for 30 minutes. Meanwhile, line an extra-large cookie sheet with parchment paper; set aside.

2 Preheat oven to 300°F. Add the vanilla and cream of tartar to the egg whites. Beat with an electric mixer on medium speed until soft peaks form (tips curl). Gradually add sugar, 1 tablespoon at a time, beating on high speed until stiff peaks form (tips stand straight) and sugar is almost dissolved (about 7 minutes total). Gently fold in hazelnut liqueur.

3 Spoon meringue mixture into a decorating bag fitted with a ½-inch open star tip, filling the bag half full. Pipe 1½-inch-diameter stars about 1½ inches apart onto prepared cookie sheet, refilling

bag as necessary. Press a hazelnut into the center of each star.

4 Bake for 3 minutes. Turn off oven and let cookies dry in oven with the door closed about 45 minutes or until crisp. Peel cookies from paper.

5 In a small saucepan combine chocolate pieces and shortening; cook and stir over low heat until melted. Gently dip the bottom of each cookie into the chocolate mixture. Wipe off excess chocolate on the edge of the pan. Place dipped cookies, chocolate sides down,* on waxed paper; let chocolate set. Makes about 36 cookies.

*****Note:** If the hazelnut falls out of a cookie, use a small dab of chocolate to fasten it back in place.

To store: Place dipped cookies in layers separated by waxed paper in an airtight container; cover. Store in a cool, dry place for up to 3 days. Or place cookies in a freezer container; cover and freeze for up to 3 months.

Chocolate-Raisin and Oatmeal Cookie Mix

shown on page 49

WHAT YOU NEED

  1 cup rolled oats
  ¾ cup all-purpose flour
  ½ cup packed brown sugar
  ¼ cup granulated sugar
  ½ teaspoon baking powder
  ⅛ teaspoon baking soda
  ¼ teaspoon pumpkin pie spice or ground cinnamon
  1 cup chocolate-covered raisins
  ½ cup chopped walnuts or pecans

HERE'S HOW

1 In a clean 1-quart jar or covered container, layer oats, flour, brown sugar, granulated sugar, baking powder, baking soda, spice, raisins, and nuts. Seal jar and attach directions for making cookies; store in a cool, dry place for up to 1 month. Makes enough mix for about 36 cookies.

To make Chocolate-Raisin and Oatmeal Cookies: Preheat oven to 350°F. Line a cookie sheet with parchment paper or nonstick foil; set aside. In a large mixing bowl stir together contents of jar, ⅓ cup softened butter, 2 eggs, and ½ teaspoon vanilla until well combined (dough will be soft). Drop by rounded teaspoons 2 inches apart on prepared cookie sheet. Bake for 9 to 11 minutes or until edges are brown. Let cool on cookie sheet for 2 minutes. Transfer cookies to wire racks and let cool. Makes about 36 cookies.

Cherry-Almond Cutouts

shown on page 50

WHAT YOU NEED

- ⅔ cup butter, softened
- ¾ cup granulated sugar
- 1 teaspoon baking powder
- ¼ teaspoon salt
- 1 egg
- 1 tablespoon milk
- 1 teaspoon vanilla
- ½ teaspoon almond extract
- 2 cups all-purpose flour
- ¾ cup slivered almonds, toasted and chopped
- ½ cup snipped candied cherries
- 1 cup powdered sugar
- 3 to 4 teaspoons half-and-half, light cream, or milk
- ¼ teaspoon almond extract
  Sanding sugar

HERE'S HOW

1 In a large mixing bowl beat butter with an electric mixer on medium to high speed for 30 seconds. Add granulated sugar, baking powder, and salt. Beat until combined, scraping sides of bowl occasionally. Beat in egg, milk, vanilla, and ½ teaspoon almond extract until combined. Beat in as much of the flour as you can with the mixer. Stir in any remaining flour. Stir in almonds and cherries. Divide dough in half. Cover and chill dough 30 minutes or until easy to handle.

2 Preheat oven to 375°F. On a lightly floured surface, roll each half of the dough until ⅛-inch thick. Using a 2-inch cookie cutter, cut dough, being careful to cut through fruit and avoid jagged edges. If desired, use a fluted vegetable cutter (crinkle cutter) or fluted pastry wheel. Place 1 inch apart on an ungreased cookie sheet.

3 Bake for 7 to 8 minutes or until edges are firm and bottoms are very lightly browned. Transfer cookies to a wire rack and let cool.

4 For frosting, in a small bowl combine the powdered sugar, half-and-half, and ¼ teaspoon almond extract. Pipe frosting onto cookies in small dots. Sprinkle with sanding sugar. Let cookies stand until dry. Makes 40 cookies.

To store: Place cookies in layers separated by waxed paper in an airtight container; cover. Store at room temperature for up to 3 days. Or place unfrosted cookies in a freezer container; cover and freeze for up to 3 months. Thaw cookies and frost.

Sables

shown on page 51

WHAT YOU NEED

- 1 cup butter, softened
- 1⅓ cups powdered sugar
- ½ teaspoon baking soda
- ⅛ teaspoon salt
- 5 egg yolks
- 1 teaspoon vanilla
- 3 cups all-purpose flour
- 1¼ cups finely chopped candied fruit
  Light-colored corn syrup, optional
  White nonpareils, optional
- 1½ cups powdered sugar
- 2 tablespoons hot water

HERE'S HOW

1 In a large mixing bowl beat butter with an electric mixer on medium to high speed for 30 seconds. Add the 1⅓ cups powdered sugar, the baking soda, and salt. Beat until fluffy. Beat in egg yolks, one at a time, beating on low speed and scraping bowl after each addition. Beat in vanilla. Gradually beat in flour just until combined. Stir in candied fruit.

2 Divide dough into thirds. On a lightly floured surface, roll each portion into a 9-inch log. If desired, brush logs with corn syrup and roll in nonpareils. Wrap logs in plastic wrap and chill for 3 hours or overnight.

3 Preheat oven to 350°F. Cut each log into about thirty-two ¼-inch slices; place slices ½ inch apart on ungreased cookie sheets. Bake for 9 to 10 minutes or until edges are golden brown.

4 Place a large wire rack over a sheet of waxed paper. For icing, in a small bowl combine the 1½ cups powdered sugar and water until smooth. Immediately transfer the warm cookies to the wire rack. Drizzle tops with icing while cookies are warm; let cool completely. Makes about 96 cookies.

To store: Place cookies in layers separated by waxed paper in an airtight container; cover. Store in a cool, dry place for up to 3 days. Or place cookies in a freezer container; cover and freeze for up to 3 months.

Create **Candy Wreath Ornaments**, *opposite*, with purchased candies and pretty sheer ribbons. Design your own **Cozy Candy Cottage**, *above*, any way you like to suit everyone in the family. Instructions are on *pages 64–65*.

Sweet dreams are close at hand with these delightful holiday decorating ideas.

visions of
sugarplums

Make a sweet forest of **Candy-Stripe Topiary Trees and Lollipops.** White fondant colored with soft Christmas hues is swirled together to make the magical trees. A grouping of lollipops makes a colorful centerpiece or use individually as package toppers. Instructions are on *page 65*.

Soft textures and dreamlike colors make **Marshmallow Magic,** *above* and *opposite,* in no time. Use purchased colored marshmallows to create the ornaments and garland. The **Pastel Candy Canes**, *opposite bottom*, are surprisingly simple to make using oval gumdrops and snippets of wire. Make all the candy trims and hang in a white feather tree. Instructions for the sweet ornaments are on *pages 66–67*.

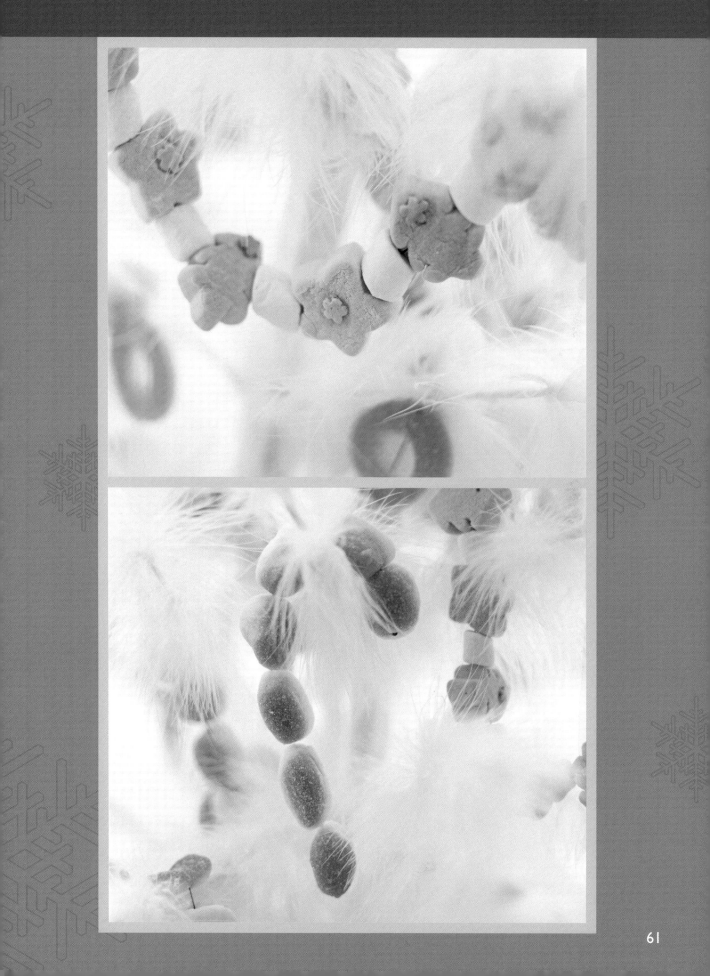

Placed on a window ledge, **Cookie-Cutter Light Catchers,** *above*, glisten like stained glass. The sparkling trims are made by melting hard candies into metal cookie cutters. **Sugar Snowflakes,** *opposite*, are created using sugar cubes and a bit of glue—no two are ever alike. Instructions for all of the projects are on *page 67*.

Candy Wreath Ornaments

shown on page 57

WHAT YOU NEED

3-inch diameter tart pans without
    removable bottoms; baking sheet
Nonstick cooking spray
Assorted hard candies; assorted colors
    and widths of sheer ribbon; scissors

HERE'S HOW

1 Preheat oven to 325°F. Place tart pans
on a baking sheet. Coat each tart pan with
nonstick cooking spray. Place five or six
pieces of hard candy around edge of each
tart pan, leaving a hole in the middle.
2 Bake 4 to 5 minutes or until individual
candy pieces just begin to melt together.
Remove from oven. Place tart pans in the
freezer about 3 minutes or until slightly
warm, but not cold and brittle.
3 Invert pans and remove wreaths by
applying pressure on the back of each pan
with both thumbs. Loop sheer ribbon
through wreath centers to hang.

Cozy Candy Cottage

shown on page 56

WHAT YOU NEED

Graph paper and pencil or copy machine
Three 24-ounce packages of vanilla-flavor
    candy coating (additional will be
    needed for Candy-Coated Cone Trees)*
Heavy saucepans, medium and small
Scissors; small, sharp knife; spoon
Foil; large spoon; baking sheet, optional
Round pastel mints, licorice-flavor
    candies, fruit-flavor candy canes,
    and other assorted hard candies
Small heavy resealable plastic bags

HERE'S HOW

1 Enlarge the patterns, *below*, onto graph
paper, or use a copy machine to reach the
desired size. The house shown, *right*, stands
about 11 inches tall and 8½ inches deep.
Cut out patterns.
2 Melt candy coating, 1 pound at a time,
in a medium heavy saucepan over low
heat. Pour each batch of melted coating
onto a 20×12-inch piece of foil on a smooth
surface. Spread coating to ⅛ to ¼ inch
thick. Holding edges of the foil, gently
shake to smooth coating. (If you don't
have a smooth work surface, place the foil
on a baking sheet; shake sheet and foil
together.) For roof pieces crush hard
candies; sprinkle onto coating on foil while
coating is soft. Let stand 15 to 30 minutes
until set. Or refrigerate for 3 minutes.
3 Place pattern pieces on top of cooled
coating. Cut around pattern with a small,
sharp knife. Reheat scraps of coating
(except candy-sprinkled roof pieces) and
repeat steps above to make remaining
pieces. When cool, peel foil from the
pieces. Place pieces on waxed paper.
4 To decorate front, back, and sides of
house, melt remaining candy coating
scraps into a small heavy saucepan over
low heat. Place coating in a small heavy

plastic bag; seal. Snip one corner of the
bag to make a small opening. Working in
small areas, pipe the coating onto the
house pieces where candy decorations are
desired. Place candies in coating and let
set. (If coating hardens in the plastic bag
as you work, place bag in the microwave
oven and heat on high about 30 seconds.)

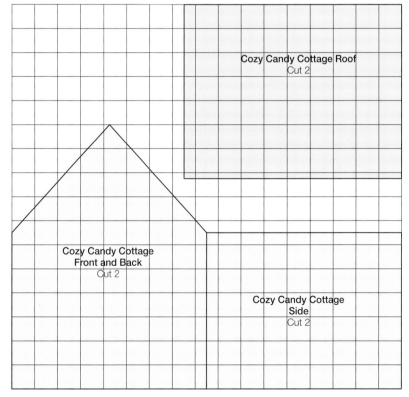

1 Square = 1 Inch
Enlarge at 400%

5 To assemble the cottage, pipe coating along one short side of one side piece; attach to front piece. Hold pieces in place about 1 minute. Repeat with remaining side and back pieces. When four walls are set, attach roof pieces in same manner. If desired, attach straight candy canes at roof peak.

6 For Candy-Coated Cone Trees melt 8 ounces of vanilla-flavor candy coating in a small heavy saucepan over low heat. Spoon coating over pointed ends of rolled sugar ice cream cones. Sprinkle with colored sugar or press candies into coating. Let cool until set.

*Note: If sheets of cooled candy coating seem hard and crumble when cut, remelt with 1 or 2 teaspoons shortening. Be careful not to overheat. Use a knife to trim pieces that don't fit exactly, or simply remelt the coating and cut a new piece.

Candy-Stripe Topiary Trees and Lollipops

shown on pages 58–59

WHAT YOU NEED

24-ounce box of ready-to-use white fondant (available where cake-decorating supplies are sold)*

Paste food coloring in green, pink, or purple; knife

Yardstick; plastic wrap

Hot-glue gun and glue sticks

8- to 10-inch-tall plastic foam cones for trees

Hard candies; decorative container

8-inch lollipop sticks; gumdrops, optional

HERE'S HOW

1 Be prepared to work quickly to prevent fondant from drying out. Cut off one-fourth of fondant. Knead in small amount of food coloring and shape into an 8-inch-long log. Set aside. Cut remaining white fondant in half. Shape halves into 8-inch-long logs.

2 Cut all three fondant logs in half lengthwise, making six logs. Place a colored log between two white logs and press together to form one log that has a strip of color through the center (see photo, *above*). Holding ends of the log, gently twist. Repeat with the remaining logs.

3 Working with one twisted log at a time, roll fondant on a large, flat surface to create a thin, swirled rope about 36 inches long. Cut the rope in half and continue to twist and roll each rope piece to 36 inches. After twisting and rolling fondant, you should end up with four 36-inch ropes about ½ inch in diameter; keep covered with plastic wrap until ready to use.

4 For topiary tree use a low-temperature glue gun to avoid melting the plastic foam and apply glue to the bottom 2 inches of a cone. Beginning at the bottom, carefully wrap one fondant rope around the cone (see photo, *above*). Continue to glue and wrap until the cone is covered, using new ropes as needed. Let stand at least 1 hour to dry. To finish, hot-glue a hard candy to the treetop. Place tree in a container. If desired, decorate base with gumdrops.

5 For the lollipop shape one fondant rope into a triangle or circle, beginning in the center. (Or, beginning at the top, make a tree shape by zigzagging the rope with each row longer than the previous row.) Moisten the ends of the rope with water, then gently press to the shape to seal. Insert a lollipop stick several inches into the bottom of the shape. Let stand at least 1 hour to dry.

*Note: One 24-ounce box of fondant will make one large topiary tree and one lollipop, or eight lollipops and no tree. Although fondant is edible, these projects are intended for decorating only. The trees use glue and shouldn't be eaten. Because the lollipops have thicker rolls of fondant, which is traditionally rolled out into a very thin layer on cakes, it won't be too tasty.

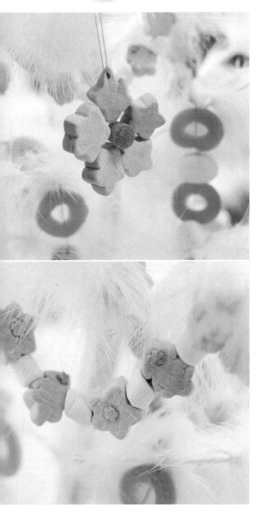

HERE'S HOW

1 Cut five 1½-inch pieces of wire. At one end, twist the wires together using pliers until secured together. Bend the wire ends outward like spokes on a wheel.
2 Push a gumdrop onto the twisted wire center being careful so the wires do not poke through the candy.
3 Push a shaped marshmallow onto each wire spoke.
4 Poke a hole in the tip of one marshmallow. Cut a 5-inch piece of cording. Thread cording through hole in marshmallow. Knot the cording ends to create a hanger.

Marshmallow Magic
shown on pages 60–61

WHAT YOU NEED
for the garland
Waxed paper
Marshmallows in holiday shapes, such as trees and stars in green and pink
Miniature white marshmallows
Flower-shape decorative sprinkles in pink and green
Crafts glue
Scissors
Fine wire

HERE'S HOW
1 Lay marshmallows on waxed paper in the desired arrangement. Glue a sprinkle on each green and pink marshmallow shape. Let dry.
2 Cut a length of wire the desired length of garland. String the marshmallows onto the wire, alternating the pink and green shapes and placing a white marshmallow between each shape. When the garland is complete, loop the wire ends to secure the marshmallows.

WHAT YOU NEED
for the ornaments
Crafting wire; wire snips
Pliers
Small gumdrops in red and green
Marshmallows in holiday shapes, such as trees and stars in green and pink
Fine silver cording
Large sewing needle

Pastel Candy Canes
shown on page 61

WHAT YOU NEED
Medium crafting wire; wire snips
Ruler; round-nose pliers
Pink oval or multicolor gumdrop candies

HERE'S HOW
1 For each ornament cut an 8-inch length of wire. Bend the wire into a candy-cane shape, forming a small hook on one end using pliers.

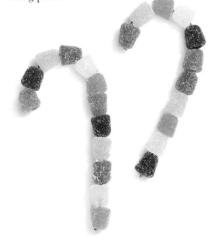

2 Thread gumdrops onto the straight end of the wire. When the wire is full, bend a hook into the straight end of the wire.

Cookie-Cutter Light Catchers
shown on page 63

WHAT YOU NEED
Metal cookie cutters
Assorted bright, translucent hard candies
Small heavy resealable plastic bags

HERE'S HOW
1 Preheat oven to 325°F. Place the cookie cutters onto a foil-lined baking sheet. If desired, coat inside of cutters with nonstick cooking spray so candy can be removed from cutters after baking.

2 Sort candies by color into separate plastic bags; seal. Cover with a kitchen towel and coarsely crush candies using a hammer or meat mallet. Transfer crushed candies to small bowls.

3 Spoon the crushed candies into cookie cutters, forming a single layer of candy about ¼ inch thick. If desired, mix colors to make designs in the cookie cutters.

4 Bake 4 minutes or until candies begin to melt. Do not overbake. Cool before removing from the foil and, if desired, from cutters.

Sugar Snowflakes
shown on page 62

WHAT YOU NEED
Waxed paper
Sugar cubes in various shapes
    (available at grocery stores)
White crafts glue
Fine silver cording
Scissors

HERE'S HOW
1 Lay a piece of waxed paper on a flat surface. For each ornament arrange the sugar cubes to form the desired shape on waxed paper.
Note: Sugar cubes are often found as square cubes, but they are also available in playing card suit shapes.

2 Using a drop of the white crafts glue, glue the sugar shapes together wherever they touch. Allow to dry.

3 Cut a length of silver cording and slip it through one of the holes between the sugar shapes. Knot the ends to make a loop for hanging.

stitch it up

Whether you love to knit, quilt, embroider, cross-stitch, or machine-sew, you'll find fun and festive ideas galore.

Cast on and knit some **Striped Mittens**, *above*, for yourself or someone special on your Christmas list. The mittens work up quickly using chunky wool yarn. Create **Partridges in a Fir Tree**, *right*, with a little felt and some pretty embroidery stitches. Each feathered friend has a personality all its own. Instructions are on *pages 78–79*.

Cross-stitch rustic **Cabin Ornaments**, *above*, in no
time to hang as special trims on your evergreen this year.
Then make some **Pretty-as-a-Postcard Stockings**,
opposite, using a clever iron-transfer method and your
favorite image. Instructions for both projects are on
pages 79–82.

Quilt a little **Calico Pieced Pot Holder**, *above*, that will brew

up Christmas spirit in your kitchen. Make an extra one to give

to a neighbor or friend. You'll be ready to celebrate carrying

a **Raspberry-Color Cabled Purse**, *opposite*, that you knit.

Instructions for the projects are on *pages 82–83*.

Decorative little **Yuletide Yo-Yos**, *below*, add your personal
touch to any package. Choose the favorite holiday motif that suits
you. And for your table, stitch up a **Snow Gals and Pals Table
Mat**, *opposite*. The cute little snow-person motif is repeated for
multiple fun. Instructions for the projects are on *pages 84–85*.

Oh-so-lovely **Satin Rosette Ornaments**, *above*, can be used on the tree or on a special package. Make them in colors that suit your holiday color scheme. **Pretty Purse Ornaments**, *opposite*, lend fashionable flair to the branches. Instructions for the projects are on *pages 85–89.*

Striped Mittens
shown on page 68

SKILL LEVEL Easy
SIZES Adult size S (MEDIUM, L)

FINISHED MEASUREMENTS
Width: 3¾ (4¼, 5)"
Length: 10 (10½, 11¼)"

WHAT YOU NEED
Lion Brand Yarn Company,
 Wool-Ease Chunky, Article #630,
 80% acrylic/20% wool yarn (153
 yards per ball): 1 ball each of
 Huckleberry (139) for A, Concord
 (145) for B, Bluebell (107) for C, and
 Charcoal (152) for D
Size 6 (4.25mm) knitting needles or size
 needed to obtain gauge
Size 4 (3.5mm) knitting needles
Yarn needle
2 ring-type stitch markers

GAUGE
In St st (k RS rows, p WS rows) with larger
needles, 16 sts and 23 rows = 4"/10cm.
TAKE TIME TO CHECK YOUR GAUGE.

SPECIAL ABBREVIATIONS
M1: To make 1 st, lift the horizontal bar
between right and left needles onto the
left needle, and k into back of this lp.
Ssk: Slip next 2 sts knitwise, one at a
time to right-hand needle, insert tip of
left-hand needle into fronts of these 2 sts
and k tog.
Pm: Place a marker.

STITCHES USED
Stripe Pattern (any multiple; a rep of
18 rows)
Row 1 (WS): P with A.
Row 2: K with A.
Rows 3–4: Rep Rows 1–2.
Row 5: Rep Row 1.
Row 6: K with D.
Rows 7–11: Rep Rows 1–5 with B.
Row 12: K with D.
Rows 13–17: Rep Rows 1–5 with C.
Row 18: K with D.
Rows 1–18 form Stripe Pattern.

HERE'S HOW
FIRST MITTEN
With color A and larger needles, cast on
25 (29, 35) sts. Work Stripe Pattern Rows
1–5. Inc 1 st each edge now, and then
every 4th row twice more—31 (35, 41)
sts. Cont in est pattern to approx 2½ (3,
3½)" from beg, ending with a WS row.

Thumb (Cont in Stripe Pattern)
Row 1 (RS): K 15 (17, 20), pm, M1, k1,
M1, pm, k 15 (17, 20).
Row 2: P across.
Row 3: K to marker, sl marker, M1, k to
marker, M1, sl marker, k to end of row.
Rep Rows 2–3 until there are 13 (13, 15)
sts bet markers. P 1 row.
Next Row: K across, removing markers
and placing thumb sts onto a spare strand
of yarn. Cont in stripes on the 30 (34, 40)
sts until piece measures approx 8½ (9,
9½)" from beg, ending with a WS row and
pm after 15th (17th, 20th) st.

Top Shaping (Cont in Stripe Pattern)
Row 1 (RS): Ssk, k to 2 sts before marker,
k2tog, sl marker, ssk, k to last 2 sts,
k2tog.
Row 2: P across.
Rep Rows 1–2 until 18 (18, 20) sts rem.
P across. (K2tog) across. P9 (9, 10).
Leaving a long tail for sewing, cut yarn.

Closure
Thread tail into yarn needle. Beg with the
last st on needle, take yarn back through
rem sts, twice. Pull up to tightly close
opening. Join sides tog.

Thumb (Cont in Stripe Pattern)
With RS facing, return sts to larger needle.
Join correct yarn color and k13 (13, 15).

Next Row: P5 (5, 7), p2tog, p6. Work 6
(6, 8) more rows in Stripe Pattern on the
12 (12, 14) sts. (K2tog) across. Cut yarn,
leaving a 10" tail. Rep Closure as for Top.
Join thumb seam. Darn opening. Weave
in loose ends on WS of fabric.

SECOND MITTEN
Work as for First Mitten.

Partridges in a Fir Tree
shown on pages 68–69

WHAT YOU NEED
Tracing paper; pencil; scissors
Felt in red, purple, gold, turquoise,
 and black; ruler
Embroidery floss in black, lime green,
 red, turquoise, purple, and orange
Sewing needle; straight pins
¼-inch-wide black satin ribbon; fiberfill

HERE'S HOW
1 Trace the patterns, *opposite*, onto tracing
paper; cut out. From desired colors of felt,
use patterns to cut a pair of wings and
bird shapes. Cut a 1½-inch square of felt
for the head feathers. Fold the square in
half and make ½-inch-long cuts into the
fold, approximately ⅛ inch apart. Cut
three ¼-inch-wide strips from black felt:
two 8 inches long and one 16 inches long,
piecing if needed.
2 Using running stitches, sew a short black
felt strip to each wing piece, allowing a
narrow border of black to show around the
edge. Embellish the wing as desired using
French knots, straight stitch, lazy daisy, or

other desired decorative stitches as shown on *page 157*. While stitching, tack each rounded wing section to a bird body piece, aligning the front and back. Make a French knot eye on both the front and back of the bird bodies.

3 Fold the fringed head feathers in half and pin to the wrong side of one bird head piece. Cut a 13-inch piece of ribbon; fold in half. Pin the tails to the center back of one bird body. Use running stitches to sew the front to the back, sandwiching the remaining black felt strip between the layers and sewing through the head feathers and ribbon ends. Before the piece is entirely stitched, stuff with fiberfill; stitch closed. Sew the wing tips together.

Cabin Ornaments
shown on page 71

WHAT YOU NEED
8-inch square of 10-count natural
    cross-stitch fabric; needle
The Thread Gatherer's Sheep's Silk in
    the colors listed in key
Iron; scissors
Self-stick mounting board; ruler
Tracing paper; pencil
Extra-loft fleece; felt; fabric glue

⅓ yard of ⅜-inch-wide flat braid
⅓ yard of twisted cord; jingle bell

HERE'S HOW
1 Center and stitch the desired chart, *page 80*, on the fabric. Work the cross-stitches over one square of the fabric with one strand of thread. Use two strands of thread to backstitch. Press the finished design from the back.

2 For the square and rectangle ornaments, cut mounting board ½ inch larger all around than the stitched design. Trace the heart shape on the pattern sheet onto tracing paper, cut out the pattern, and use the pattern to cut one heart from mounting board. Use the mounting board shape to cut the fleece and felt.

3 Peel the protective paper from the mounting board. Center and adhere the sticky side on the fleece. Trim the fleece even with the board edges. Center the stitched piece on the fleece side of the mounting board. Trim excess fabric to ¾ inch beyond the board; fold extending fabric to the back and glue it in place.

4 Position and glue flat braid around the ornament edge. Fold the twisted cord in half and glue the fold to the center top on the back of the mounting board. Knot each loose cord end. Glue felt to ornament back. Sew a jingle bell to the cord base.

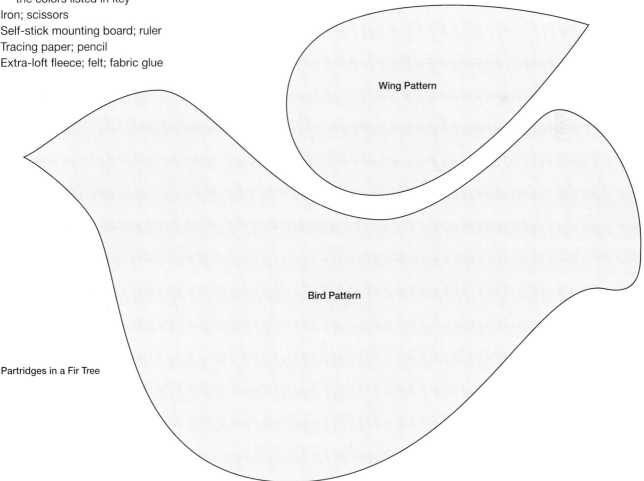

Wing Pattern

Bird Pattern

Partridges in a Fir Tree

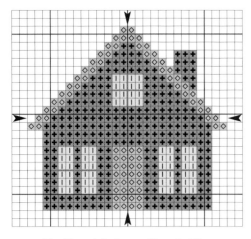

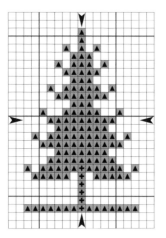

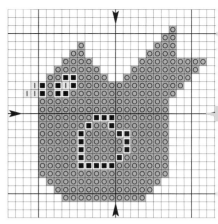

The Thread Gatherer–Sheep's Silk
CROSS-STITCH (2X)
◇ SPS 073 Cocoa brown
✚ SPS 078 Autumn twilight
Ⅰ SPS 145 Maple bisque
BACKSTITCH (2X)
／ SPS 078 Autumn twilight –
windows
Stitch count: 45 high x 104 wide
Finished design size:
10-count fabric– 4¹/₂ x 10³/₈ inches

The Thread Gatherer–Sheep's Silk
CROSS-STITCH (2X)
▲ SPS 039 Dark forest
✚ SPS 078 Autumn twilight
Stitch count: 23 high x 15 wide
Finished design size:
10-count fabric– 2¹/₃ x 1¹/₂ inches

The Thread Gatherer–Sheep's Silk
CROSS-STITCH (2X)
◯ SPS 020 Ruby red
■ SPS 050 Ink black
Ⅰ SPS 145 Maple bisque
Stitch count: 22 high x 24 wide
Finished design size:
10-count fabric– 2¹/₄ x 2³/₈ inches

Pretty-as-a-Postcard Stockings

shown on page 70

WHAT YOU NEED
for either transfer stocking
Vintage postcards
Photo transfer paper for fabric
Tracing paper; pencil; scissors
½ yard of 54-inch-wide wool fabric
with smooth finish suitable for
photo transfer
½ yard of 45-inch-wide lining fabric
Sewing machine; thread; sewing needle
1½ yards of sew-in piping cord
¼ yard of white wool for photo transfer
for cuff; yardstick

HERE'S HOW
to construct either stocking
1 Photocopy the postcard in color,
increasing the size as desired. Photocopy
the image onto photo transfer paper.
2 Enlarge and trace the pattern, *opposite*;
cut out. Use the patterns to cut a stocking
front, back, and two lining pieces.
3 For noncuff version transfer the photo
onto the wool fabric according to the
manufacturer's instructions, referring to
the photograph, *right*, for placement.

4 Stitch piping around the stocking front
sides and foot. Right sides facing, stitch
the stocking front to back using a ½-inch
seam. Clip the seam and turn.
5 For cuff cut a 6½×16½-inch rectangle
from white wool and lining fabric with
design transferred to center of wool. Stitch
the short ends together for each piece.
Turn to the right side. Right sides facing
and matching seams, stitch the lining to
the cuff along bottom edge. Clip seam and
turn to right side. Baste the cuff to the
stocking top edge. Make a fabric hanging
loop; stitch it to cuff at the stocking back.
6 Stitch the lining pieces together, leaving
an opening for turning. Slip the stocking
into the lining with right sides facing. Stitch
around the top edge. Pull the stocking
through the lining opening. Stitch the lining
closed. Hand-press the lining to the inside.

WHAT YOU NEED
for front transfer stocking
½ yard of white novelty tinsel trim
½ yard of ⅜-inch-wide red grosgrain
ribbon with metallic rickrack stitched
on top
½ yard of ½-inch-wide novelty velvet
ribbon lace trim

Gold metallic machine thread
Thin layer of quilt batting the size of
stocking front

HERE'S HOW
1 Line the stocking front with batting and
machine-quilt in gold thread around the
transfer design. Assemble the stocking
according to the general instructions,
page 80, omitting the cuff. Hand- or
machine-stitch trims around the top edge
of the stocking.

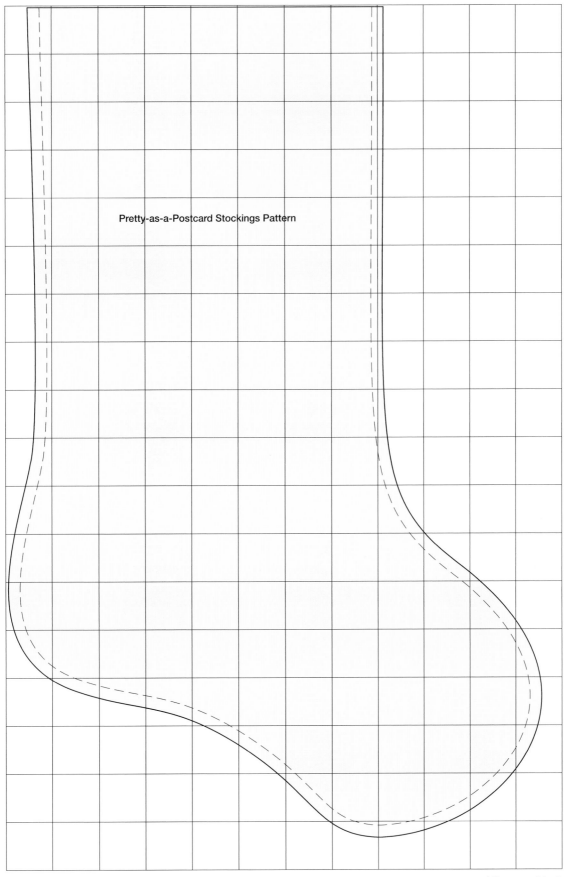

Pretty-as-a-Postcard Stockings Pattern

1 Square = 1 Inch
Enlarge at 200%

WHAT YOU NEED

for cuff transfer stocking

½ yard of ⅜-inch-wide red and gold flat braid

½ yard of ½-inch-wide green pom-pom bead trim

1 yard of ½-inch-wide grosgrain ribbon

Two 2-inch-long gold tassels

HERE'S HOW

1 Assemble the stocking according to the general instructions, *page 80*, with the design transferred to the cuff.

2 Trim the edge of the cuff by hand- or machine-stitching trims in place. Add a bow and tassels to the top of the cuff.

Calico Pieced Pot Holder

shown on page 72

WHAT YOU NEED

Tracing paper; pencil; scissors

⅛ yard each of 2 different red calico fabrics

⅓ yard green calico fabric for piecing and backing

Sewing machine; thread; sewing needle

Batting

Embroidery floss in red and green

1-inch cabone ring
12mm green wood bead

HERE'S HOW

1 Trace the pattern pieces, *below*; cut out. Use the patterns to cut pieces from calico, using the photo as a color guide.

2 Piece the calico fabrics according to the diagram, *below*. Layer quilt top, batting, and backing. Quilt the pad as desired.

3 Bind the pot holder edge with red fabric. Tie the pot holder if desired using green embroidery floss.

4 Single crochet over the cabone ring using red embroidery floss. Slip the ends of the floss through the bead and attach the ring to the pot holder.

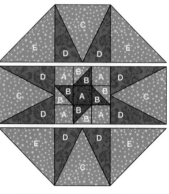

Pot Holder Assembly Diagram

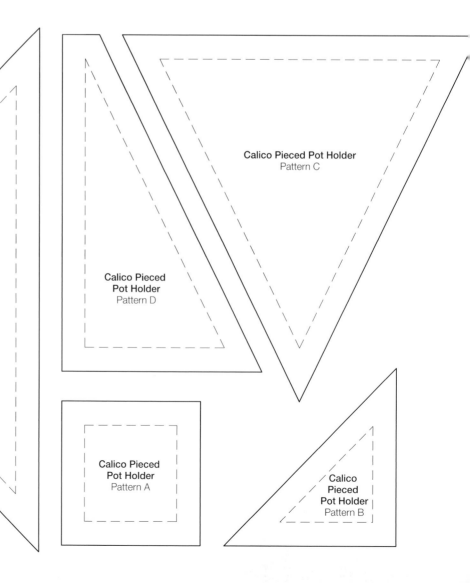

Calico Pieced Pot Holder
Pattern E

Calico Pieced
Pot Holder
Pattern D

Calico Pieced Pot Holder
Pattern C

Calico Pieced
Pot Holder
Pattern A

Calico Pieced
Pot Holder
Pattern B

Raspberry-Color Cabled Purse

shown on page 73

Purse measures approximately 13 inches wide by 9 inches deep.

WHAT YOU NEED

Caron International's Simply Soft 100% acrylic yarn (6 ounces per skein):
  1 skein Raspberry for MC (9723) and
  1 skein Dark Country Blue for CC (9711)
Size 8 (5 mm) knitting needles or size to obtain gauge
Cable needle (cn)
One size F/5 (3.75mm) crochet hook
Tapestry needle
2 handbag ring-handles
1 yard of ¼-inch-wide ribbon to match MC
Row counter, optional
Stitch markers, optional

SPECIAL TECHNIQUE

M1–Lifted increase: Insert RH needle into the top of the stitch one row below the stitch on LH needle from the back; place loop on LH needle and knit it, then knit stitch on LH needle. This causes the fabric to move to the right. To move the fabric to the left, insert the LH needle into the top of the stitch two rows below the one just worked on the RH needle (this is the same row as before, but you have already worked the stitch above), knit the loop, then continue.

STITCHES USED

Stockinette stitch (St st)
Single crochet (sc)

Eyelets

* K2tog, yo, k3; repeat from * across, beg and end as indicated.

Cable (see Chart)

Read RS rows from right to left, WS rows from left to right; check the Key carefully. This cable pattern contains working methods that may vary from conventional patterns.

GAUGE: In Stockinette stitch, 18 sts and 24 rows = 4"/10cm.
Gauge is not critical for this project.
HELPFUL: Place a marker between each 16-st repeat of Chart.

HERE'S HOW
OUTER PURSE (Make 2)

Using MC, cast on 54 sts; purl 1 row.

Establish Pattern

Beginning Row 3 of Chart, work first 16 sts, work 16-st repeat twice, work to end. Work even until piece measures 8" from beg; end with a WS row.

Eyelet Row: K3; work Eyelets across to last st; k1.
Work even in St st for 7 rows.
Repeat Eyelet Row.
Purl 1 row even.
Bind off all sts.

LINING

Using CC, CO 52 sts; purl 1 row.

Eyelet Row: K2; work Eyelets across, end last repeat, k2.
Purl 1 row even.

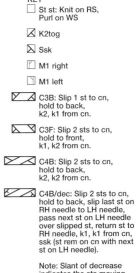

Decrease Row: K2tog, knit across to last 2 sts, K2tog—50 sts remain.
Purl 1 row even.
Repeat last two rows—48 sts remain.
Work even in St st until piece measures 13" from beg, end with a WS row.

Increase Row: K1, M1, work across to last st, M1, k1—50 sts.
Purl 1 row even.
Repeat last two rows—52 sts.
Work Eyelet Row.
Purl 1 row even.
Bind off all sts.

FINISHING
Join Outer Pieces

With WS of pieces held tog, beg 1½ inches below the Eyelet Row on one side; work 1 row sc through both pieces, down the side, across the lower edge, then up the remaining side, joining 2 pieces tog; end 1½ inches below Eyelet Row.

Edging

Work 1 row sc along openings above Eyelets on both sides.

Join Lining Piece

Fold lining in half, eyelet rows aligned; work as for Outer pieces.
Using tapestry needle, weave in ends.

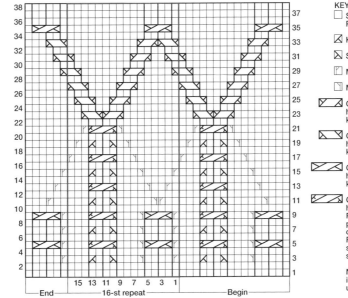

KEY
☐ St st: Knit on RS, Purl on WS
K2tog
Ssk
M1 right
M1 left
C3B: Slip 1 st to cn, hold to back, k2, k1 from cn.
C3F: Slip 2 sts to cn, hold to front, k1, k2 from cn.
C4B: Slip 2 sts to cn, hold to back, k2, k2 from cn.
C4B/dec: Slip 2 sts to cn, hold to back, slip last st on RH needle to LH needle, pass next st on LH needle over slipped st, return st to RH needle, k1, k1 from cn, ssk (st rem on cn with next st on LH needle).

Note: Slant of decrease indicates the sts moving under the cable.

ASSEMBLE PURSE

Place Lining inside Outer Purse with wrong sides together. Lay purse flat, with Eyelet edges facing toward you.

Attach Handles

Place one Handle inside Purse on top of Lining; wrap outer edge over Handle, aligning Eyelets. Thread ribbon through Eyelets (all 3 layers) to attach handle. Repeat for other handle.

Yuletide Yo-Yos

shown on page 74

WHAT YOU NEED
for the Snowman Ornament

Tracing paper; pencil; scissors
Scrap white fleece; sewing needle
Thread in white and orange
Scrap colored fleece
Scrap orange felt
Black embroidery floss
2 black glass E beads
Three 4mm square beads

HERE'S HOW

1 Trace patterns for yo-yos using the circle patterns on *page 22*. From white fleece, make one each, 2-inch yo-yo (finishing to 1-inch size), 3-inch yo-yo (finishing to 1½-inch size), 4-inch yo-yo (finishing to 2-inch size). To make a yo-yo, sew a running stitch around the edge of the circle and pull thread tight. There is no need to turn the raw edge when gathering; fleece fabric does not ravel.

2 Position the smallest yo-yo halfway over the top of the medium-size yo-yo and stitch together by hand, taking a couple of stitches through both circles. Overlap first two yo-yos halfway over the largest yo-yo, tacking together with a few hand stitches.

3 Cut slits in ends of small strip of colored fleece to fringe ends of scarf. Tie around neck, between smallest and middle circles. Sew on black beads for eyes and square beads for buttons. Sew mouth with black embroidery floss using stem outline stitch. Tack on orange felt nose using matching thread.

4 Sew thread to top through smallest circle to hang.

WHAT YOU NEED
for the Wreath Ornament

Scraps green cotton fabric
Ruby glass spacer beads
¼-inch metallic ribbon trim
Sewing thread
Green and red thread to hand-sew

HERE'S HOW

1 Make five 3-inch yo-yos (to finish to 1½-inch size). Sew yo-yos together in a circle, overlapping one over the next.

2 Embellish with ruby glass spacer beads for holly. Tie small bow and tack to wreath bottom. Sew thread through top to hang.

WHAT YOU NEED
for the Tree Ornament

Scraps of green cotton fabric
Scraps of gold/brown cotton fabric
One 12mm star bead
Amber glass spacer beads
Matching threads to hand-sew
Yarn trim for garland
Thread to hang

HERE'S HOW

1 Make six 3-inch green yo-yos (to finish to 1½-inch size) and tack together three, overlapping halfway for the bottom of the tree. Add two yo-yos to the middle and one on top to form a triangular tree shape, tacking together using several hand stitches.

2 Sew one 3-inch gold/brown yo-yo (to finish to 1½-inch size). Center trunk yo-yo in the middle of the bottom row of green yo-yos, overlapping the tree shape halfway over the gold yo-yo. Tack, using several hand stitches.

3 Sew star bead to top yo-yo. Embellish tree by sewing on glass spacer beads and yarn garland, stitching down by hand.

4 Sew thread to top to hang.

Snow Gals and Pals Table Mat

shown on page 75

WHAT YOU NEED

Tracing paper
Pencil; scissors
Felt in white, red, green, orange, and black
Ruler
Straight pins
Embroidery floss in turquoise, black, and white
Sewing needle
Assorted buttons, sequins, and beads

HERE'S HOW

1 Trace the patterns, *opposite* and on *page 86*, enlarging if necessary; cut out. Use the patterns to cut out six snowmen heads and bodies from white felt, three top hats from red felt, three stocking caps from green felt, and the white and black backing pieces. For scarves cut ¾×4½-inch felt pieces; fringe the short ends.

2 Pin the large white felt circles in a ring onto the black felt. Position and pin smaller white circle heads in place.

3 Use blanket stitches, as shown on *page 157*, and three strands of turquoise embroidery floss to attach the white circles to the black felt. Blanket-stitch the hats onto the heads using three strands of white floss, alternating the shapes. Stitch a carrot nose on each snowman head. Make French knot eyes and smiles on each head using black floss, as shown on *page 157*.

4 Sew two beads onto each snowman body to resemble buttons and trim the hat brims or points with buttons, sequins, and beads as desired.

5 Tie a knot in the center of each scarf piece. Hand-sew a scarf below each snowman's head, alternating colors.

6 Place the black cutout onto the white felt cutout and blanket-stitch in place.

**Snow Gals and Pals
Table Mat**

Nose

Hat 1

Hat 2

Snowman Body

Snowman Head

Satin Rosette Ornaments
shown on page 76

WHAT YOU NEED
Satin fabric strips: 2½×28 inches
   for rosettes; thread; sewing needle
Green satin fabric: 2½×4 inches
   for leaves; felt scraps

HERE'S HOW
Note: The following directions are for a 2½-inch rosette. For a smaller rosette reduce cutting measurements; for a larger rosette increase cutting measurements proportionately. The finished rosette is as wide as the original cut strip of fabric.

1 For rosette: With wrong sides together, fold the 2½×28-inch strip in half lengthwise. Gather the raw edges, stitching

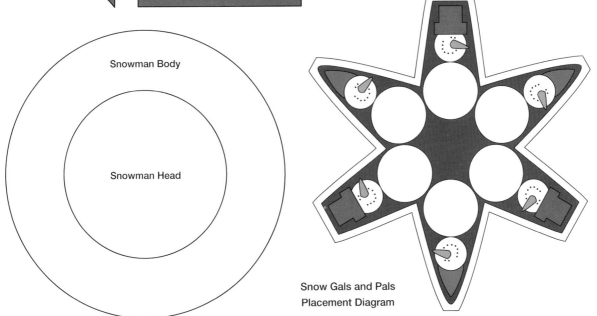

**Snow Gals and Pals
Placement Diagram**

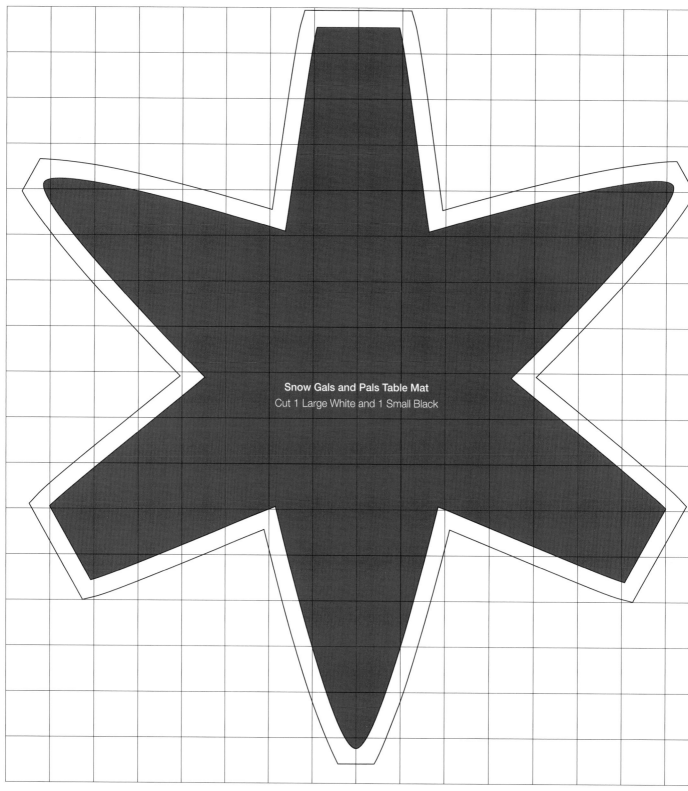

Snow Gals and Pals Table Mat
Cut 1 Large White and 1 Small Black

1 Square = 1
Enlarge at 2

across short ends in an arch to round the corners. Trim excess fabric at ends. Roll one of the rounded ends tightly toward the center to make the center of the rosette. Continue to coil the fabric around the center piece, tacking gathers together with needle and thread.

2 For leaves: With wrong sides together fold the 2½×4-inch strip in half lengthwise. Gather the raw edges, angling stitching to round the corners. Trim excess fabric at ends. Pull threads together and tie together to secure leaf shape.

3 Attach the leaves to the bottom of the rosette, tacking them in place with needle and thread.
4 Cut a 2-inch circle from felt and stitch onto back of rosette to cover fabric edges and help rosette keep its shape.

Pretty Purse Ornaments

shown on pages 77, 87, and 88

WHAT YOU NEED

for the red decorative button ornament
Tracing paper
Pencil; scissors
Red felt; ruler
Metallic gold beaded string
Sewing thread
Metallic gold embroidery floss
Large decorative button

HERE'S HOW

1 Enlarge and trace pattern A, *page 89*; cut out. Use pattern to cut one shape from red felt. Fold bottom edge up about 3¾ inches. Cut beaded string to desired length and knot a loop in the center. Tack ends of beaded string to top edges of purse, taking a couple of stitches over the end bead between layers of felt.

2 Using *page 157* for reference and three strands of metallic embroidery floss, whipstitch over edges of purse starting at the lower folded edge, continuing around top flap to other side of bottom folded edge. Cut a buttonhole slit. Using two strands of floss, sew buttonhole stitch around cut edges. Sew button to top layer of purse underneath buttonhole.

WHAT YOU NEED

for the green and gold purse ornament
Tracing paper
Pencil
Scissors
Scrap of olive green felt; ruler
Metallic gold embroidery floss
Button, zipper pull, or bauble

HERE'S HOW

1 Enlarge and trace pattern B, *page 89*; cut it out. Use the pattern to cut one shape from green felt.

2 Fold up purse bottom 1⅞ inches. Use all 6 strands of metallic embroidery thread to make handle. Knot ends and place between layers of felt at top edges.

3 Using two strands of gold metallic thread, buttonhole stitch up one side, around scalloped flap, and down remaining side. Attach desired button, zipper pull, or bauble at center of flap.

WHAT YOU NEED

for the vertical ribbon purse ornament
Tracing paper
Pencil
Scissors
Scrap light green felt; ruler
Straight pins; matching thread
⅞-inch decorative ribbon
Needle; gold cording
Metallic gold embroidery floss
½-inch shell button

HERE'S HOW

1 Enlarge and trace pattern C, *page 89*; cut it out. Use the pattern to cut one shape from light green felt.

2 Fold up bottom about 3 inches and mark top fold line where flap folds to the front. With felt laying flat, pin ribbon down the center front, extending the length ¼ inch beyond the top fold line and over the other edge. Fold raw edges of ends under ¼ inch and tack ribbon to felt using matching thread and an invisible hand stitch. Fold bottom edge up 3 inches and pin sides together. Attach a 6-inch-long gold cording handle at sides by tacking with several hand stitches between felt layers. Using two strands of metallic floss, sew running stitch around outside edges.

3 Make a buttonhole in top flap, sewing buttonhole stitch with matching thread. Sew button underneath buttonhole using two strands metallic floss, attaching to front edge of purse only.

WHAT YOU NEED

for the woven ribbon flap ornament
Tracing paper
Pencil
Scissors; iron
Green felt
⅜-inch satin ribbon in lime green, dark green, and red
Sewing thread; needle; ruler
Green embroidery floss

HERE'S HOW

1 Enlarge and trace patterns D and D1, *page 89*; cut out. Use patterns to cut one of each shape from green felt.

2 Weave ribbons (as described on *page 19*) on top of piece D1. Baste around outside edges. On one long edge turn ribbon ends to underside and hand-tack in place. With right sides together, stitch woven section to piece D, stitching around sides and front long edge, using narrow ⅛-inch seam. Turn to outside and press lightly. Hand-stitch open woven edge to felt back. Fold flap to front, creasing and pressing top edge so that about ½ inch of the ribbon remains to the back.

3 Fold up bottom edge of green felt 3¼ inches. Cut a ribbon handle to desired length, insert at sides, and sew along both side edges, tacking down with a few hand stitches. Sew along both side edges, using running stitches and three strands of floss sewn through both thicknesses.

WHAT YOU NEED
for the lime green ornament
Tracing paper
Pencil
Scissors
Lime green felt; ruler; straight pins
Red and lime green cording
Sewing thread; needle
Red suede yarn
Awl
4mm square beads in red, green and gold

HERE'S HOW
1 Enlarge and trace pattern E, *opposite*; cut out. Use pattern to cut one shape from lime green felt. Fold up bottom edge 3½ inches and pin side edges together. Insert double cording handles between layers of felt at top edge where flap is to fold over. Tack down, taking several hand stitches.

2 Using running stitch, stitch through both thicknesses along side edges, around top flap curve, and around remaining side edge. This ornament was stitched using a thick suede yarn and holes were punched through felt layers using an awl to ease yarn through both layers of felt. It also can be stitched using several strands of embroidery floss or Perle cotton.

3 Sew beads in center of top flap. Lightly press at top fold.

WHAT YOU NEED
for the beaded-handle purse ornament
Tracing paper
Pencil
Scissors
Scrap of cream felt; ruler; straight pins
Micro bead mix in gold and red
Gold metallic thread
Cream-colored embroidery floss
⅜-inch snap
½-inch pearl button

HERE'S HOW
1 Enlarge and trace pattern F, *opposite*; cut it out. Use the pattern to cut one shape from cream felt.

2 Fold bottom up 2⅜ inches and pin at sides. Thread beads onto metallic thread to make approximately a 6-inch length. Knot ends. Attach beaded handle to sides, slipping between felt layers at top edges. Tack down with several hand stitches.

3 With three strands embroidery floss, blanket-stitch around edges, starting at lower side, around flap, and around final side. Sew snap to top flap in right corner and to top of purse front. Using metallic thread, attach button on top of snap, ending with long thread. String beads onto thread before knotting ends.

WHAT YOU NEED
for the red fringed bottom purse
Tracing paper; pencil
Scissors
Red glitter felt; ruler
Bead fringe trim; thread; sewing needle
Red cording
Red eyelash yarn
Red embroidery floss
Crochet hook

HERE'S HOW
1 Enlarge and trace pattern G, *opposite*; cut out. Use pattern to cut one shape from red glitter felt. Fold bottom edge up about 3½ inches. Cut felt along bottom fold. Insert bead fringe between layers of felt and sew right sides together in a narrow ⅛-inch seam. Turn to outside. Sew cording handle to top edge between layers of felt, tacking down with a couple of stitches.

2 Crochet a chain 6 to 8 inches long using eyelash yarn. Sew chain of yarn to edge of flap, tacking down with sewing thread. Trim fringes just a bit to shorten.

3 Using three strands of red embroidery floss, sew buttonhole stitch around side edges, through both layers, continuing along the single layer of the flap. Fold down top edge of flap to front.

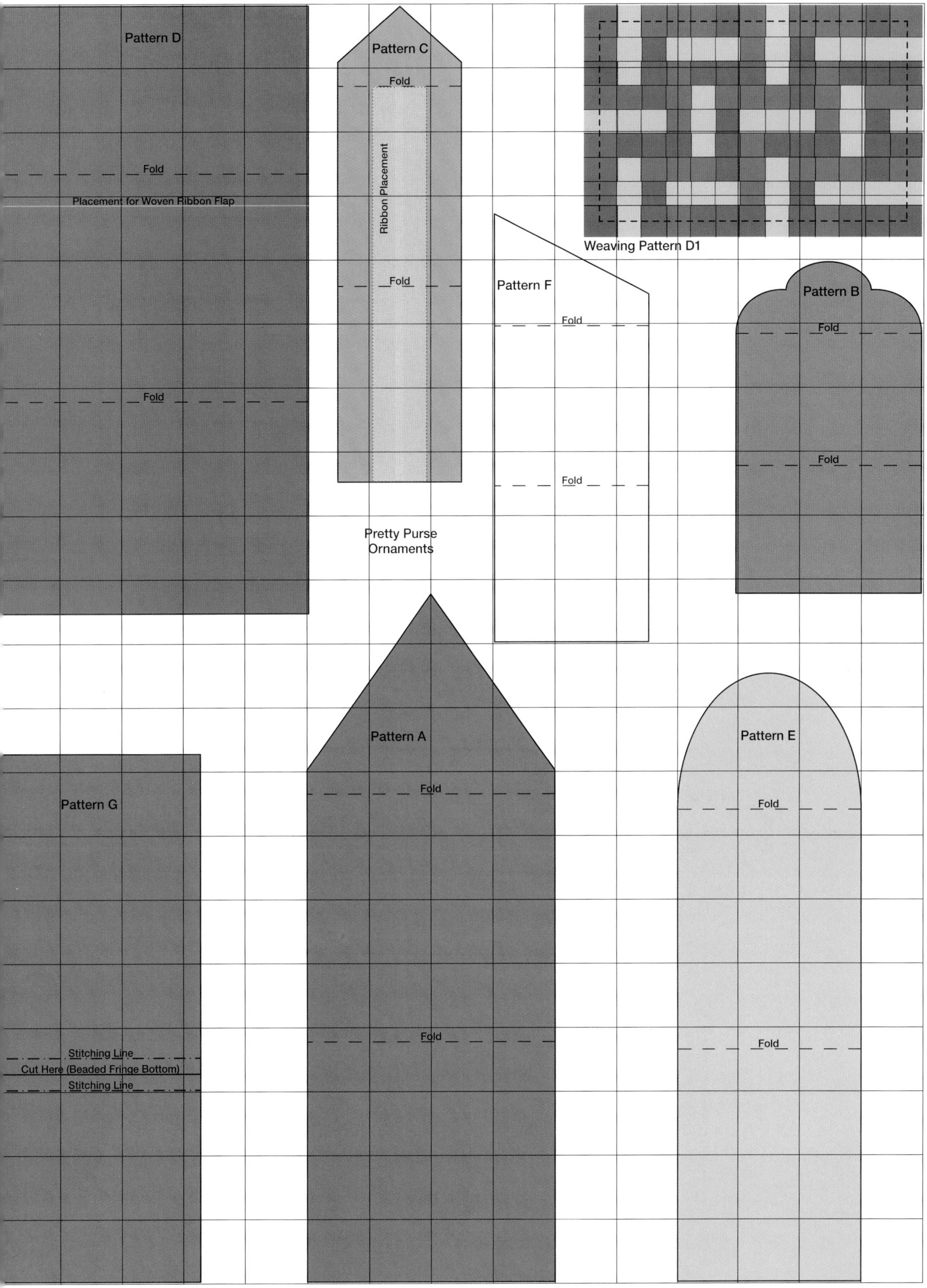

Pattern D

Fold

Placement for Woven Ribbon Flap

Fold

Pattern C

Fold

Ribbon Placement

Fold

Weaving Pattern D1

Pattern F

Fold

Pattern B

Fold

Fold

Fold

Pretty Purse
Ornaments

Pattern G

Pattern A

Fold

Pattern E

Fold

Stitching Line
Cut Here (Beaded Fringe Bottom)
Stitching Line

Fold

Fold

1 Square = 1 Inch
Enlarge at 200%

MAY EVERY HOUR OF CHRISTMASTIDE
BRING HAPPINESS TO YOU

Keep the holidays happily organized with lovely containers to hold all the surprises and supplies of the season.

everything
in its place

Embellish a plain wood box and turn it into a

Gilded Greetings Box to hold your special greeting

cards. The box has applied wood corners and a tassel,

and opens to display a vintage card. Instructions

are on *page 96*.

Wrapping gifts will become merrier when you use a **Holiday Hold-It-All**, *left*. Start with a simple wicker hamper and add pockets for all your wrapping essentials. Pick your favorite hues of disc cases and turn them into **Colorful Catchalls**, *below*, to keep desk supplies handy.

Little purchased containers become **Helpful Boxes**, *far left*, that make

a big difference in organizing tiny office supplies. Use alphabet stickers

for labeling and you are set! Keep treasured ornaments safe by making

a pretty **Diamond Window Ornament Box**, *above,* to store them

after the holidays. Instructions for all projects are on *pages 96–97*.

93

Perfect for yourself or as a gift, the **Tote-It Sewing Bag**, *opposite,* is made from colorful cotton and has pockets inside and out. Make Christmas card writing easy this year by keeping supplies in a clever **Card-Writing Kit,** *below.* Pretty embossed felt is used for the outside, while vinyl pockets inside hold the tools needed. Instructions are on *pages 97–99.*

Gilded Greetings Box

shown on pages 90–91

WHAT YOU NEED

Unpainted wood box with hinged lid,
    approximately 9×12 inches
Fine sandpaper; tack cloth; newspapers
Spray sanding sealer
Outdoor opaque acrylic paint, such as
    Plaid Folk Art, in fresh foliage,
    engine red, pure gold metallic,
    and emerald green metallic
Paintbrush
Four 3½-inch-square wood ornament
    corner medallions
Vintage postcard photocopied in size
    to fit inside lid; scissors
Decoupage medium
Extra-fine steel wool; wood glue
Four 1-inch wood finishing buttons
Spray acrylic varnish
⅝-inch brass finish knob
2-inch gold tassel

HERE'S HOW

1 Sand the box and wipe away the dust
with a tack cloth. In a well-ventilated
work area, cover the surface with
newspapers. Spray the box with sanding
sealer; let dry.
2 Paint the box and wood medallions
using the photo as a guide for color
placement. Let the paint dry.
3 Trim the postcard photocopy to fit the
underside of the lid. Decoupage the
photocopy onto the lid according to the
manufacturer's instructions. If using more
than one coat, sand with steel wool
between coats.

4 Glue a wood finishing button in each
corner of the box bottom for legs. Glue
the medallions onto the lid.
5 In a well-ventilated work area, cover
work surface with newspapers. Spray the
box with acrylic varnish; let dry.
6 Attach the knob and tassel to lid center.

Colorful Catchall

shown on page 92

WHAT YOU NEED

Hot-glue gun and glue sticks
5 HD discs in red, yellow, green, purple,
    and blue

HERE'S HOW

1 Hot-glue the edges of the four discs
together to form the shell of a box. Glue
the remaining disc on one end to form the
box bottom.

Helpful Boxes

shown on page 92

WHAT YOU NEED

Purchased small colorful boxes
    (available at scrapbook stores)
Small stickers (alphabet and other)

HERE'S HOW

1 Place stickers on boxes as desired, spelling
words that fit the contents of the boxes.

Holiday Hold-It-All

shown on page 92

WHAT YOU NEED

Tape measure
White wicker hamper with hinged lid
Scissors; 1-inch-wide foam
Perforated Peg-Board to fit inside
    hamper lid
Upholstery spray adhesive
Batting; sewing machine; thread
¼-inch diameter red braided cord
⁵⁄₃₂×1½-inch cotter pins; awl
1½ yards of 45-inch-wide red print
    fabric
1 yard of 45-inch-wide green
    contrasting fabric
¼ yard of 54-inch-wide clear vinyl
3 yards of red ⅞-inch-wide double-fold
    bias quilt binding
3 yards of green ½-inch-wide
    double-fold bias quilt binding
3 yards of red and white check 1-inch-
    wide double-fold bias quilt binding

HERE'S HOW

1 Cut layers of foam to fill the inside of the lid. In a well-ventilated work area, spray-adhere the foam inside lid. Cut perforated Peg-Board slightly smaller than the inside lid measurement. Cut green fabric 1 inch larger than the Peg-Board measurement. Spray adhesive onto a layer of batting and press onto the outside of the Peg-Board. Spray-adhere green fabric to batting, wrapping and gluing extra fabric to the back.

2 String lengths of red braided cord through the cotter pins. Use an awl to pierce a hole in the fabric. Insert cotter pins into Peg-Board from the front to the back and spread prongs to secure. In a well-ventilated work area, spray-adhere the Peg-Board to the foam inside lid.

3 Measure the depth and width of the hamper. To cut the length of the red fabric, add the width of the hamper to the two depth measurements and add seam allowances. To cut the width of the red fabric, measure the inside height of the hamper and add the thickness of the rim, plus 6½ inches for the fold-over cuff and seam allowances. For the liner back piece, measure the height and width of the hamper and add seam allowances; cut green fabric to these measurements.

4 To make the clear vinyl pockets, cut vinyl 6 inches longer than the width of the red fabric minus the seam allowance. Bind the top edge of the vinyl with red bias binding. Matching and centering bottom edge of vinyl to edge of red fabric, stitch vertical lines where desired to create four pockets. Trim seam allowance from red fabric at ends of vinyl. Bind sides and bottom edge of pockets with green bias binding.

5 For hamper bottom, cut a rectangle from green fabric to fit, adding seam allowances.

6 Bind top edge of green fabric liner with red and white check binding. Stitch red pocket piece to green liner back along back seams. Stitch green bottom piece to bottom of liner, easing in fullness of liner to bottom. Topstitch two 30-inch lengths of red check bias binding to make ties. Fold ties in half crosswise, then fold up bottom edge to create a point. Stitch ties to lining back at lid hinge placement. Slip ties through lid and tie around the hinges to secure.

Diamond Window Ornament Box

shown on page 93

WHAT YOU NEED

Photo box
Newspapers; gold spray paint
Decorative scrapbook papers
Scissors
Double-sided tape
Spray mount
Crafts knife; ruler
Black marking pen
Hot-glue gun and glue sticks
Gold rope trim
Clear sheet of transparency
Solid color card stock

HERE'S HOW

1 Set the box lid aside. In a well-ventilated work area, cover the work surface with newspapers. Spray-paint the outside and inside of the box bottom. Let dry.

2 Cut strips of paper to fit around the edges of the lid. Adhere the strips to the lid with spray mount or double-sided tape. Adhere decorative paper to the top of lid. Trim excess paper with crafts knife.

3 Cut diamond shapes out on top of the lid using a crafts knife. Apply black marking pen to the inside edges of the diamond shapes. Hot-glue gold rope trim to the diamond edges. (**Tip:** For a cleaner look, hot-glue the start of the trim and end of trim from the back side of lid.) Adhere a piece of transparency to the back side of the lid using double-sided tape.

4 Cut a piece of decorative paper and secure it to the bottom of the box. Cut some additional squares of paper and decorate the sides and ends of the box. Fold one piece of solid-color card stock in half. Trim it to fit inside the long side of the box. Fold another piece of solid card stock and trim two pieces of it to fit crosswise inside the box. Cut midway down the center of the two folded pieces that fit crosswise. Cut two slits from the bottom of the folded card stock that fits the long side. Cut and adjust until the card stock pieces fit together to form a grid. Insert into the box bottom.

Card-Writing Kit

shown on page 95

WHAT YOU NEED

Scissors; ½ yard of 72-inch-wide red embossed felt
⅓ yard of 54-inch-wide clear vinyl
Pinking shears; thread sewing needle
2 yards of ¾-inch-wide red novelty ribbon
2 yards of 1-inch-wide red belting
6 yards of ⅝-inch-wide red and white stripe ribbon
⅓ yard of 2-inch-wide red elastic
14×36-inch piece of cotton quilt batting
Cabone ring
Two ½-inch-wide color snaps
8½×11-inch green cutting board with handle
Two 1¾-inch red star buttons

HERE'S HOW

1 Cut the following:

- Two 14×36-inch pieces of red felt
- 9×10-inch piece of vinyl
- Two 2×10-inch pieces of vinyl for flaps, rounding edges as shown, *above*
- Two 12×10-inch pieces of vinyl

2 Layer the felt pieces wrong sides together and trim even with pinking shears. Work outside and inside pieces of felt separately. For handles topstitch the red novelty ribbon onto red belting, then topstitch to outside as shown in diagram, *opposite top*.

3 Bind inside round edges of vinyl flaps with striped ribbon. Bind sides and bottom edge of vinyl pockets with striped ribbon. For center pocket bind top edge of vinyl. To give depth to center pocket, stitch ribbon singly along sides and bottom of vinyl, then stitch to felt. Topstitch pockets and flap to inside of felt according to diagram. Topstitch red elastic above small pocket, wrong sides facing with batting between, topstitch outside and inside felt together around outside edge. Make vertical stitches to separate compartments.

4 Add snaps to pockets and flaps according to the manufacturer.

5 Add two rows of topstitching centered between pocket sections. Stitch a 24-inch piece of red stripe ribbon in half lengthwise for ties. Fold in half and stitch ties centered at side edge opposite handle. Stitch the cabone ring centered between the small and center pockets.

6 Insert card-writing supplies into the pockets and elastic. To close, fold the organizer in thirds, securing first section with ribbon through cabone ring. Fold

remaining section matching handles. Add star buttons to the outside at the bottom edge of the handle.

Tote-It Sewing Bag

shown on page 94

WHAT YOU NEED

Scissors

$7/8$ yard of multicolored fabric, medium to heavy weight, such as poplin or denim

1 yard blue fabric, medium to heavy weight, such as poplin or denim

Matching sewing thread

Fusible webbing

WHAT TO CUT

From multicolored fabric:

Cut one piece $18\frac{1}{2}$ inches wide (cross grain of fabric) × 30 inches long (lengthwise grain of fabric) for outside of bag

Cut 2 pieces 7 inches long (lengthwise grain of fabric) × 9 inches across (crosswise grain of fabric) for inside pockets

Cut scrap appliqué shape from print, if desired, for pocket decoration

From blue fabric:

Cut one piece $18\frac{1}{2}$ inches wide (cross grain of fabric) × 30 inches. long (lengthwise grain of fabric) for inside lining of bag

Cut one piece $18\frac{1}{2}$ inches wide (cross grain of fabric) × $9\frac{3}{4}$ inches long (lengthwise grain of fabric) for bottom trim of bag

Cut 2 pieces $5\frac{1}{4}$ inches wide × $7\frac{1}{2}$ inches for outside pockets

Cut 2 pieces 3 inches wide × 34 inches long for handles

HERE'S HOW

1 To prepare pockets for front, press under $\frac{1}{4}$ inch on upper edge. Press upper edge to inside again $\frac{3}{4}$ inch, to form facing. Stitch close to folded edge, about $\frac{3}{4}$ inch from top edge. Use fusible webbing to fuse decorative shape to center of pocket and sew around shape with zigzag appliqué stitch. Pin wrong side of pocket over right side of outside multicolored fabric, centering folded edges of pockets $4\frac{1}{2}$ inches from short edges. Baste raw edges to bag.

2 To sew handles and bottom section, fold handles in half lengthwise with right sides together. Stitch long edges. Turn handle right side out, bringing seam to center on underside; press. Pin underside of handles to bag (over pockets), having raw edges of handles and pockets even. Stitch close to

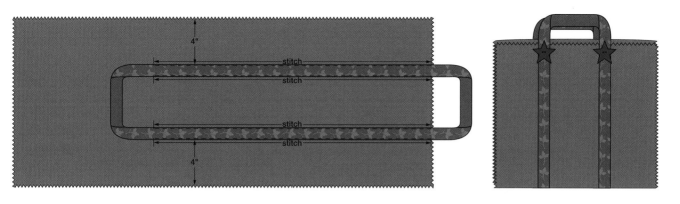

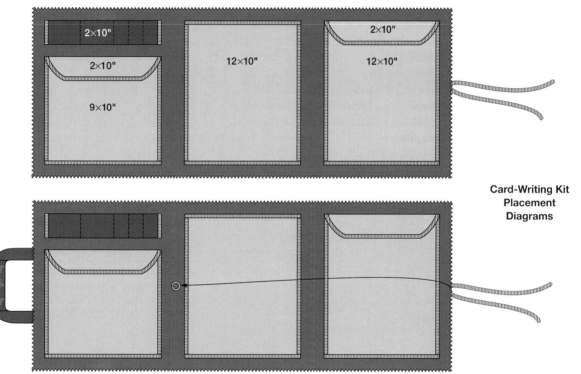

**Card-Writing Kit
Placement
Diagrams**

long edges of handles, to within 2½ inches of edge of bag, backstitching to secure.

3 Press under ⅝ inch on long edges of bottom blue section of fabric. Pin wrong side of bottom section over right side of multicolored bag, covering raw edges of pockets and handles. Stitch close to long edges, catching pockets and handles. Baste side edges together.

4 Fold bag with right sides together. Stitch side edges using ⅝-inch seams and press open. Press under ⅝ inch on upper edges of bag.

5 To prepare facing, press in ½ inch around side and bottom edges of lining pockets. Press upper edge to inside ¼ inch. Press upper edge to inside again ¾ inch, to form facing. Stitch close to folded edge, about ¾ inch from top edge. Place pocket on blue lining piece, 3½ inches down from upper

raw edge of bag. Attach pocket to lining, sewing close to side and bottom edges. Sew down center of one pocket, through pocket and lining fabric to divide the pocket into smaller organizational sections.

6 Stitch seams of facing, and press under upper edge same as for bag.

7 Turn bag inside out. At bottom of bag, fold the fabric point to match up with the seam line of the bottom blue section, creating a triangle to measure 3 inches from the point. Stitch perpendicular to the side seam, forming a line to add depth to the bottom of the bag. Do the same with the blue lining section.

8 With wrong sides together pin facing to bag with upper edges even. Stitch upper edges together, close to folds. Turn bag right side out.

party
goodies

*With this creative collection
of festive dips, sippers,
and appetizers, you can treat
family and friends to the
best party bites ever.*

When you want to pull out all the stops, tuck a

luscious spread into some gorgeous **Gougères**,

opposite. **Frisky Sours**, *above,* can be made in spiked

and unspiked versions—either makes an exuberant

way to kick off an evening. Recipes are on *page 110.*

Sweet and Salty Nuts, *left,* are great for gift-giving, but save some for your holiday entertaining, too. Gather around the Christmas tree with steaming cups of **Alpine-Style Hot Chocolate,** *above,* and some of your favorite cookies. Recipes are on *pages 110–111.*

Cheese stars in two irresistible ways. Your guests will rave about **Brie with Winter Fruit Conserve**, *above*—a most seasonal take on the fruit-and-Brie combo. **Bruschetta with Goat Cheese**, *opposite*, brings a windfall of color to the spread. Recipes are on *page 111.*

Treat guests to the bold flavors of **Mojo Chicken Wings**

with Mango Sauce, *above.* **Cheese Triangles,** *opposite,*

bake up irresistibly crisp and puffy. Recipes are on *page 112.*

German Meatballs with Lemon-Caper Sauce, *far left*, bring an elegant angle to a favorite standby. What's a party without a great dip? Zippy Cheddar-Jack Cheese Dip, *above*, and Spinach Salad Dip, *below*, will do you proud as they disappear fast. Recipes are on *pages 112–113*.

Gougères

shown on page 100

WHAT YOU NEED

1½ cups water
½ cup unsalted butter, cut into pieces
1½ cups all-purpose flour
5 eggs
1½ cups shredded Gruyère cheese (6 ounces)
4 teaspoons Dijon-style mustard
⅛ teaspoon ground white pepper
⅛ teaspoon cayenne pepper

HERE'S HOW

1 Preheat oven to 400°F. Lightly grease two baking sheets; set aside. In a medium saucepan combine water, butter, and ½ teaspoon salt. Bring to boiling. Add flour all at once, stirring vigorously. Cook and stir until mixture forms a ball. Remove from heat. Transfer to a large mixing bowl. Cool 10 minutes. Add eggs, one at a time, beating with an electric mixer on medium speed for 1 minute after each addition. Stir in Gruyère cheese, mustard, white pepper, and cayenne pepper.

2 Drop batter in 1-inch mounds about 1½ inches apart onto the prepared baking sheets. Bake for 30 to 35 minutes or until puffed, golden brown, and firm. Cool on a wire rack. Fill with desired filling. Makes about 60 puffs.

Make-Ahead Directions: Bake and cool puffs as directed. Place puffs in an airtight container and refrigerate up to 24 hours.

Gougères with Cucumber Filling

shown on page 100

WHAT YOU NEED

½ of an 8-ounce package cream cheese, softened

½ of an 8-ounce package soft goat cheese (chèvre)
½ teaspoon fresh lemon juice
1 medium cucumber, peeled, seeded, and finely chopped (¾ cup)
2 tablespoons finely chopped radish
2 tablespoons finely snipped fresh dill
2 teaspoons finely chopped green onion
¼ teaspoon salt
Dash cayenne pepper
1 recipe Gougères (see recipe, *left*)

HERE'S HOW

1 In a medium mixing bowl combine cream cheese, goat cheese, and lemon juice. Beat with an electric mixer on medium speed until smooth. Stir in cucumber, radish, dill, green onion, salt, and cayenne pepper; mix well. Cover and chill for 1 to 2 hours to blend flavors.

2 Meanwhile, prepare Gougères; cool. Cut Gougères in half horizontally with a serrated knife. Spoon cucumber filling into the bottom half of each puff. Replace tops. Serve immediately or cover and chill for up to 2 hours. Makes about 1½ cups filling (enough for 60 Gougères).

Gougères with Tuna Mousse Filling

shown on page 100

WHAT YOU NEED

2 6-ounce cans tuna packed in olive oil, drained
½ cup unsalted butter, softened
¼ cup olive oil
1 teaspoon finely shredded lemon peel
2 tablespoons fresh lemon juice
2 teaspoons minced shallot
¾ teaspoon dried thyme, crushed
½ teaspoon salt
¼ teaspoon ground black pepper
1 recipe Gougères (see recipe, *left*)

HERE'S HOW

1 In a food processor combine tuna, butter, olive oil, lemon peel, lemon juice, shallot, thyme, salt, and pepper. Cover and process until smooth and airy. Transfer to a bowl; cover and chill filling for 1 to 2 hours to blend flavors.

2 Meanwhile, prepare Gougères; cool. Cut Gougères in half horizontally with a

serrated knife. Spoon tuna filling into the bottom half of each puff. Replace tops. Serve immediately or cover and chill for up to 2 hours. Makes about 2 cups filling (enough for 60 Gougères).

Frisky Sours

shown on page 101

WHAT YOU NEED

¾ cup frozen lemonade concentrate, thawed
⅓ cup frozen grapefruit juice concentrate, thawed
⅓ cup frozen orange juice concentrate, thawed
1½ cups whiskey, optional
1½ cups cold water
Crushed ice

HERE'S HOW

1 In a blender combine juice concentrates, whiskey (if using), and water. Cover and blend until frothy. Serve over crushed ice. Makes eight (about 4-ounce) servings.

Sweet and Salty Nuts

shown on pages 102–103

WHAT YOU NEED

Butter
1 pound walnut pieces or pecan halves (about 4½ cups)
½ cup granulated sugar
⅓ cup light-colored corn syrup
1 tablespoon coarse sea salt or kosher salt or 2 teaspoons salt
½ teaspoon freshly ground black pepper
Coarse raw sugar

HERE'S HOW

1 Preheat oven to 325°F. Using about 2 tablespoons butter, generously butter a 15×10×1-inch baking pan; set aside. In a large bowl stir together the nuts, granulated sugar, corn syrup, salt, and pepper until well combined; spread in prepared pan.

2 Bake for 25 minutes or until golden and bubbly, stirring once or twice. Remove from oven. Sprinkle generously with raw sugar; toss to coat. Transfer mixture to a large piece of foil. Cool completely, about 30 minutes. Break apart to serve. Makes 20 to 24 (about ¼-cup) servings.

To store: Store in an airtight container at room temperature up to 2 weeks or freeze in a freezer container up to 3 months.

Alpine-Style Hot Chocolate

shown on page 103

WHAT YOU NEED

- 4 cups milk
- ½ cup water
- ½ cup sugar
- 8 ounces bittersweet or semisweet chocolate, coarsely chopped
- 1 recipe Schlag, optional*
  English toffee, crushed, optional
  Unsweetened cocoa powder, optional

HERE'S HOW

1 In a medium saucepan combine milk, water, and sugar. Stir over medium heat until mixture just comes to a boil. Remove from heat. Stir in chocolate. Beat with an immersion blender, rotary mixer, or whisk until chocolate is melted and mixture is frothy.

2 To serve, pour hot chocolate into cups. If desired, top with Schlag, crushed English toffee, and cocoa powder. Serves 4 to 6.

*Schlag: In a medium mixing bowl combine 1 cup whipping cream, 2 tablespoons sugar, and 2 teaspoons vanilla. Beat until soft peaks form (tips curl).

Brie with Winter Fruit Conserve

shown on page 104

WHAT YOU NEED

- 1 15-ounce can figs, drained and quartered
- 1½ cups chopped, peeled pears
- ¼ cup sugar
- ½ cup dried currants
- ½ cup finely chopped unpeeled orange (½ of an orange)
- ¼ cup dry red wine
- 2 tablespoons fresh lemon juice
- ⅛ teaspoon salt
- ½ cup chopped walnuts, toasted
- 1 1-pound wedge Brie or Camembert cheese

HERE'S HOW

1 For conserve, in a medium saucepan combine figs, pears, sugar, currants, orange, wine, lemon juice, and salt. Bring to boiling; reduce heat. Boil gently, uncovered, about 25 minutes or until mixture is thickened and most of the liquid has evaporated. Transfer to a bowl.

2 Cover and chill about 2 hours or until completely cool. Stir in nuts. Serve with Brie or Camembert cheese. Makes 2½ cups.

Bruschetta with Goat Cheese

shown on page 105

WHAT YOU NEED

- 1 8-ounce loaf baguette-style French bread, cut into ½-inch slices
- 3 tablespoons olive oil
- 3 ounces goat cheese (chèvre), crumbled
- 2 ounces reduced-fat cream cheese (Neufchâtel)
- 2 teaspoons lemon juice
- 1 teaspoon snipped fresh sage or oregano or ¼ teaspoon ground sage or oregano
- 1 cup bottled roasted red sweet peppers, drained
- 1 cup coarsely chopped pitted kalamata olives or ripe olives
  Fresh sage or oregano, finely shredded, optional

HERE'S HOW

1 Preheat oven to 425°F. To prepare toasts, lightly brush both sides of each bread slice with the olive oil. Arrange on an ungreased baking sheet. Bake for 10 to 12 minutes or until crisp and light brown, turning once.

2 Meanwhile, stir together goat cheese, cream cheese, lemon juice, and snipped sage. Cut red peppers into strips.

3 To assemble, spread each slice of toast with cheese mixture. Top with red pepper strips, chopped olives, and shredded fresh sage, if desired. Serve warm or at room temperature. To heat, return slices to the ungreased baking sheet. Bake in a 425°F oven about 3 minutes or until the toppings are heated through. Makes about 24.

Mojo Chicken Wings with Mango Sauce

shown on page 106

WHAT YOU NEED

- 1 cup mango nectar
- ½ cup fresh lemon juice (3 lemons)
- ½ cup fresh orange juice (2 oranges)
- ½ cup snipped fresh parsley
- ¼ cup red wine vinegar
- ¼ cup olive oil
- 1 tablespoon minced garlic (about 6 cloves)
- 1 or 2 fresh jalapeño chile peppers, seeded and finely chopped*
- 1 teaspoon salt
- ½ teaspoon ground cumin
- 2 pounds chicken wing drumettes (about 24)**
- 1 mango, seeded, peeled, and chopped
- 1 small onion, chopped
- ¼ cup chopped fresh cilantro

HERE'S HOW

1 For marinade, in a medium bowl whisk together mango nectar, lemon juice, orange juice, parsley, vinegar, oil, garlic, jalapeño, salt, and cumin. Reserve ½ cup of the marinade for sauce; cover and chill until needed. Place drumettes in a self-sealing plastic bag set in a shallow dish; pour remaining marinade over drumettes. Seal bag. Marinate in the refrigerator for 2 hours or overnight, turning bag occasionally. Drain and discard marinade.

2 Preheat oven to 450°F. Arrange drumettes in a single layer on the rack of a large broiler pan. Bake for 25 minutes or until the drumettes are no longer pink in the center and are nicely browned.

3 Meanwhile, for sauce, in a blender combine reserved marinade with chopped mango, onion, and cilantro. Cover and blend until smooth. Serve drumettes with sauce. Makes 24 drumettes.

*Note: Because hot chile peppers, such as jalapeños, contain volatile oils that can burn your skin and eyes, avoid direct contact with chiles as much as possible. When working with chile peppers, wear plastic or rubber gloves. If your bare hands touch the chile peppers, wash your hands well with soap and water.

**Note: If you can't find chicken drumettes, use 12 chicken wings. Cut off and discard wing tips or reserve for making broth. Cut each wing into 2 sections (drumettes).

Cheese Triangles

shown on page 107

WHAT YOU NEED

- 2 cups all-purpose flour
- 2 teaspoons baking powder
- ¾ teaspoon cayenne pepper, optional
- ½ teaspoon salt
- 3 tablespoons shortening
- ½ cup finely shredded sharp cheddar cheese (2 ounces)
- ¾ cup milk
- 1 tablespoon milk
- ½ cup finely shredded sharp cheddar cheese (2 ounces)

HERE'S HOW

1 Preheat oven to 400°F. Lightly grease baking sheets; set aside. In a large bowl stir together flour, baking powder, cayenne pepper (if using), and salt. Using a pastry blender, cut in shortening until the size of coarse crumbs. Stir in ½ cup cheddar

cheese. Add the ¾ cup milk, stirring just until flour mixture is moistened. If necessary, knead dough slightly in bowl. Form dough into a ball.

2 On a lightly floured surface, roll dough to a 10-inch square. Brush with the 1 tablespoon milk. Sprinkle with ½ cup cheddar cheese; press cheese lightly into dough. Cut into sixteen 2½-inch squares. Cut each square in half diagonally to make 32 triangles. Place triangles on the prepared baking sheets.

3 Bake for 12 to 15 minutes or until golden brown. Serve warm. Makes 32 triangles.

Make-Ahead Directions: Prepare and bake triangles as directed; cool. Place in an airtight container and store at room temperature for up to 2 days or freeze for up to 1 month. To serve, preheat oven to 325°F. Arrange frozen triangles on a baking sheet and heat for 6 to 8 minutes or until heated through. Serve warm.

German Meatballs with Lemon-Caper Sauce

shown on page 108

WHAT YOU NEED

- 2 eggs, slightly beaten
- ¼ cup milk
- ¾ cup soft bread crumbs
- ½ cup finely chopped onion
- ¼ cup finely chopped fresh parsley
- 2 teaspoons anchovy paste
- 1 teaspoon finely shredded lemon peel
- ½ teaspoon salt
- ½ teaspoon ground black pepper
- 2 pounds ground meat loaf mix (about 11 ounces each: pork, veal, and beef)
- 2 tablespoons butter or margarine
- 2 tablespoons all-purpose flour
- ½ teaspoon salt
- 1 14-ounce can reduced-sodium chicken broth

1 tablespoon lemon juice
1 tablespoon capers, drained
1 egg yolk
1 tablespoon dairy sour cream

HERE'S HOW

1 Preheat oven to 375°F. In a large bowl combine eggs and milk. Stir in bread crumbs, onion, parsley, anchovy paste, lemon peel, ½ teaspoon salt, and pepper. Add ground meats; mix well. Shape into 48 meatballs. Arrange in a single layer in a 15×10×1-inch baking pan.

2 Bake, uncovered, about 30 minutes or until done (an instant-read thermometer inserted into the meatballs should register 160°F). Drain off fat.

3 Meanwhile, for sauce, in a large saucepan melt butter. Stir in flour and ½ teaspoon salt. Stir in broth. Cook and stir over medium heat until thickened and bubbly. Reduce heat to low; add lemon juice and capers. Simmer, uncovered, for 10 minutes, stirring occasionally.

4 In a small bowl whisk together the egg yolk with 2 tablespoons of the sauce. Return the mixture to the saucepan; whisk the mixture to combine. Stir in sour cream. Add the meatballs, stirring gently to coat. Cook for 3 to 5 minutes until heated through. Serve with decorative wooden picks. Makes 16 appetizer servings (3 meatballs per serving).

Make-Ahead Directions: Prepare meatballs as directed in steps 1 and 2. Place in an airtight container; cover. Chill for up to 24 hours. To serve, continue as directed in step 3.

Zippy Cheddar-Jack Cheese Dip

shown on page 109

WHAT YOU NEED

4 green onions, chopped
2 tablespoons olive oil
3 tablespoons all-purpose flour
1 teaspoon ground cumin
2 cups half-and-half or light cream
1 8-ounce package cream cheese, softened
1 cup shredded cheddar cheese (4 ounces)
1 cup shredded Monterey Jack cheese (4 ounces)

1 10-ounce can diced tomatoes with green chiles
4 pickled jalapeño peppers, minced
   Coarsely chopped pickled jalapeño peppers, optional
   Chopped tomato, optional
   Sliced green onion, optional
   Finely chopped green sweet pepper, optional
   Tortilla chips and/or assorted vegetable dippers

HERE'S HOW

1 In a medium saucepan cook the chopped green onions in hot oil over medium-low heat for 2 minutes. Stir in flour and cumin; cook and stir for 1 minute. Gradually stir in half-and-half. Bring just to boiling, stirring frequently. Reduce heat and simmer, uncovered, for 1 minute more. Remove from heat. Stir in the cream cheese until melted.

2 Return pan to low heat. Gradually add cheddar and Monterey Jack cheeses, stirring until melted. Stir in undrained tomatoes with green chiles and jalapeños. Cook and stir until heated through (do not boil). Transfer to a serving bowl. If desired, sprinkle with chopped pickled jalapeños, chopped tomato, sliced green onion, and/ or finely chopped green sweet pepper before serving. Serve warm with tortilla chips. Makes 24 (¼-cup) servings.

Make-Ahead Directions: Prepare dip; cool. Transfer dip to a medium microwave-safe bowl. Cover with plastic wrap and chill for up to 24 hours. To reheat, microwave on 100 percent power (high) for 3 to 4 minutes, stirring once per minute, until heated through.

Spinach Salad Dip

shown on page 109

WHAT YOU NEED

5 slices bacon
2 cups sliced fresh mushrooms
1 small onion, finely chopped (⅓ cup)
2 cloves garlic, minced
1 tablespoon red wine vinegar
1 tablespoon Dijon-style mustard
¼ teaspoon ground black pepper
3 cups chopped fresh spinach leaves
1 3-ounce package cream cheese, softened
½ cup dairy sour cream
2 tablespoons milk
   Milk
   Bagel chips or pita crisps

HERE'S HOW

1 In a large skillet cook bacon until crisp. Drain bacon on paper towels, reserving 1 tablespoon of the bacon drippings in the skillet. Crumble 4 of the bacon slices and set aside. Crumble the remaining slice of bacon; cover and chill for garnish.

2 Cook the mushrooms, onion, and garlic in the reserved drippings over medium heat until mushrooms are tender. Stir in vinegar, mustard, and pepper. Stir in spinach; cook and stir for 30 seconds or until spinach is just wilted. Remove skillet from heat. Add cream cheese, stirring until melted. Stir in sour cream, the 2 tablespoons milk, and the 4 slices of crumbled bacon. Transfer to a serving bowl. Cover and chill for 4 to 36 hours.

3 To serve, stir dip. If necessary, stir in additional milk until mixture is of dipping consistency. Top with chilled bacon. Serve with bagel chips or pita crisps. Makes 16 (2-tablespoon) servings.

lights allaround

Craft twinkling candles and lighted arrangements that glow with the warmth of the season.

Make holiday candles as fresh as can be with a **Festive Cranberry Candle**, *opposite*. Simply surround it with fresh cranberries and slivers of lime. Wrap inexpensive battery candles with pretty scrapbook papers to make **Patterned Window Lights**, *above*. Put one in each window to welcome guests. Instructions are on *page 122*.

A simple cake plate with a dome is all you need to make

Lights Under Glass, *opposite*. The Santa motif lights make

a glowing circle of joy. Add some lights to a classy holiday

flower to make a **Lighted Poinsettia Basket**, *above*. Tucked

in among the leaves, tiny bulbs make this arrangement

sparkle. Instructions are on *pages 122* and *124*.

Dress up holiday green votives to become **Perfect Star Candles**, *above*. A linoleum tool and a little gold paint are the tricks. Tell your guest how you feel about the holidays with **Message Pillars**, *opposite*. The soft messages glow when the candles are lit. Instructions are on *pages 124–125*.

Stunningly simple, the **Metallic Marbled Pillars**,
above, can be made in any colors you like. Group
them for a dramatic effect. Fill a **Jolly Holiday Jar**,
opposite, with lights and favorite Christmas
ornaments to create a holiday mood. Instructions
are on *page 125*.

Festive Cranberry Candle

shown on pages 114–115

WHAT YOU NEED
Shallow glass dish
Purchased candle
Fresh cranberries
Fresh limes; sharp knife

HERE'S HOW
1 Set the candle into the dish. Arrange cranberries around the candle. Cut tiny slices of lime rind. Curl the rind and sprinkle among the cranberries.

Note: *Never leave burning candles unattended.*

Patterned Window Lights

shown on page 115

WHAT YOU NEED
Ruler; battery candles
Pencil; scissors
Assorted holiday papers
Double-sided tape
Tracing paper
Gold leafing pen, such as Krylon 18kt.
Transparent tape

HERE'S HOW
1 Measure and cut paper to cover the vertical portion of the battery candles. Adhere the paper to the candles using double-sided tape. Layer additional paper for added interest.
2 Trace the desired patterns, *opposite;* cut out. Use patterns to cut several candle collars out of coordinating holiday papers. Trim the edges with a gold leafing pen. Let dry. Attach the collars in various places on

the candles, layering if desired. Tape the seam of the collars in the back.

Note: *Never leave candles unattended.*

Lights Under Glass

shown on page 116

WHAT YOU NEED
3 plates to fit under lid
Glass cake plate with lid
Character or decorative holiday lights
Acrylic gems in red and green
Fresh or artificial greenery
Scissors

HERE'S HOW
1 Stack the plates and arrange the lights on the cake plate. Turn on the lights and place the lid on the plate, being careful not to pinch any of the light wires. Place gems around rim of cake plate. Tuck snippets of greenery at the base.

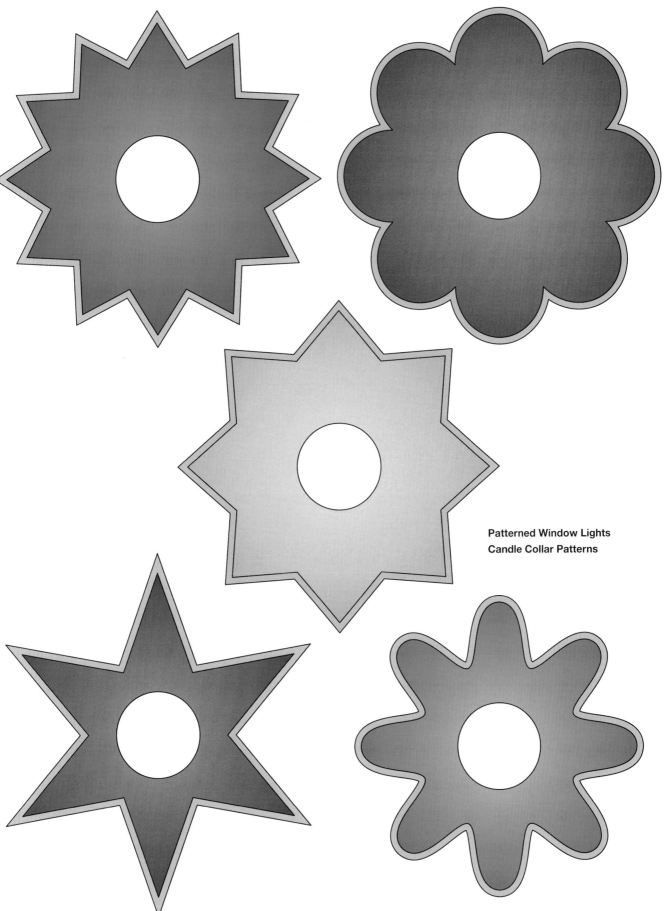

**Patterned Window Lights
Candle Collar Patterns**

Lighted Poinsettia Basket

shown on page 117

WHAT YOU NEED

Potted poinsettia plant
Lidded basket in size to hold poinsettia
50- to 100-light strand of holiday lights

HERE'S HOW

1 Place the poinsettia plant into the basket. Carefully interweave the lights with the poinsettia leaves and tuck the plug end of the cord between the basket and lid.

Perfect Star Candles

shown on page 118

WHAT YOU NEED

Pencil; small solid-color candle
Linoleum cutter; gold paint

HERE'S HOW

1 With the pencil, mark where you want the tiny stars to be carved onto the candle.
2 Using the cutter and working away from you, carve a star in the candle by first making an X and then making a line through the center of the X. Continue to make the stars on the candle following the pencil marks. Brush off any wax.
3 Using your finger, rub some gold paint into the carved area. Let dry.

Note: Never leave burning candles unattended.

Message Pillars

shown on page 119

WHAT YOU NEED

Scissors
Scrapbook paper with holiday writing
Omni-Gel; synthetic paintbrush
Small pan of water; freezer paper
Blue-purple candle sealing wax
Pillar candle; matches
Glass plate
Silver rondelle beads
Tweezers

HERE'S HOW

1 Cut a piece of holiday paper slightly larger than you plan to use for the candle design. Apply Omni-Gel to the right side of paper following the manufacturer's directions. Let dry.

2 Soak paper in water for 20 minutes and then gently remove the paper backing. Let dry flat on the slick side of a piece of freezer paper. While the image is still against the freezer paper, trim the image to the size desired. Apply a new coat of Omni-Gel to the back of the image and press onto candle surface. Let dry.

3 Light the candle sealing wax and allow the wax to drip onto the glass plate. Extinguish flame and then immediately press one rondelle bead into the mound of soft wax on the plate using a pair of tweezers. Let the wax harden. Make three additional wax-bead ornaments.

4 Lay the pillar candle on its side. Lay two heavier objects on each side of it so it won't roll. Light the candle sealing wax and allow the wax to drip onto the corner of the image on the candle. Extinguish the flame and immediately apply a wax/bead ornament to the soft wax using tweezers. Continue this process for all corners.

Note: *Never leave burning candles unattended.*

Jolly Holiday Jar
shown on page 120–121

WHAT YOU NEED
Battery-operated or plug-in
   holiday lights
Large glass jar with lid
Tree ornaments
Fresh or artificial greenery snippets

HERE'S HOW
1 Working in layers, arrange the lights, ornaments, and snippets of greenery in the jar, making the lightswitch accessible near the top of the arrangement.

2 Plug in the lights and place the lid on the jar, being careful not to pinch any of the light wires.

Metallic Marbled Pillars
shown on page 120

WHAT YOU NEED
Water
Old pan (to heat coffee can of water)
Empty, clean coffee can
Candy or candle thermometer
Newspapers

Cheese grater
Metallic crayons in purple, teal, and gold
Paper plates
Black pillar candles
Poster board
Teal and purple beads
20-gauge brass wire
Long-nose pliers
Wire snips

HERE'S HOW
1 Fill old pan one-third full of water. Fill a coffee can two-thirds full of water. Insert thermometer into coffee can water and heat to 180°F. Protect counter with newspapers. Finely grate metallic crayons one color at a time onto separate paper plates.

2 When water in the coffee can reaches 180°F, drop purple crayon shavings into the water. The crayon wax will immediately melt in the water. Dip the top one-third of a pillar candle (as evenly as possible) into the water and remove promptly. If more purple is desired on the pillar candle, add more purple crayon shavings to the water and dip again. Allow wax on the pillar to harden on paper plates or newspapers between each dipping.

3 Before melting a new color of wax, drag a piece of poster board through the water to clean the water and get rid of most of the remaining wax. Repeat with additional pieces of poster board until the water color is fairly clean. Continue melting the teal shavings and repeat the process for dipping the pillar. Finish melting the gold crayon shavings.

4 Thread desired beads onto brass wire and then wrap wire around candle pillars. Twist wire ends with long-nose pliers and cut off excess wire with wire snips.

Note: *Never leave burning candles unattended.*

Pheasant feathers and golden ornaments combine to make **Nature's Arrangement,** *above.* The color and shape of the **Artichoke Votive Holders,** *opposite,* will fit beautifully into your holiday decorating theme. With a simple cut, each holds a votive candle in the center. Instructions for both projects are on *page 134.*

nature's touch

Look to nature for your decorating inspiration. The glorious colors and textures lead to unexpected holiday beauty.

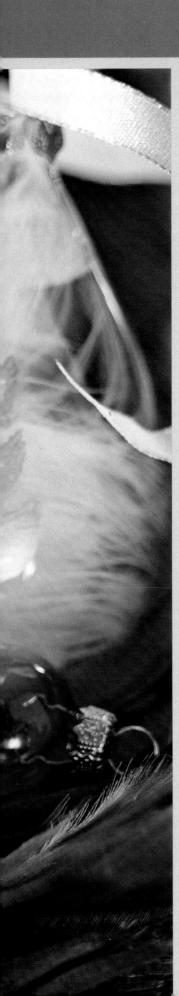

Pretty little white feathers gently touch the inside of purchased glass ornaments to create **Festive Feather Trims**, *left*. A painted motif on the front of each ornament finishes the look. Use the same simple design to deck the front of a hand-embellished gift bag. Instructions are on *pages 134–136.*

Dried dahlias look like **Flowering Snowballs**, *above*, to be used as ornaments or other decorating accents. Make a **Dried Dahlia Wreath**, *opposite*, to accompany the ornaments and complete the naturally elegant look. Instructions are on *pages 136–137*.

Turn purchased glass ornaments into **Pretty Potpourri Balls**, *below,* with little effort. Choose any color and scent to create the perfect decorating accent. Just a touch of color transforms **Color-Dipped Pinecones**, *opposite,* to fit any seasonal theme. Use them on a tree or doorknob, or as a gift trim. Instructions are on *page 137.*

Nature's Arrangement
shown on page 126

WHAT YOU NEED
Floral foam
Cutting board
Table knife
Natural-color basket
Pheasant feathers
Dried orange slices
Gold floral sprigs
Gold Christmas ornaments

HERE'S HOW
1 Place the floral foam on a cutting board. Use a table knife to cut the foam to fit the bottom of the basket.
2 Arrange the feathers by poking them into the foam. Arrange the orange slices and ornaments as desired between the feathers. Place the sprigs between the arranged items.

Artichoke Votive Holders
shown on pages 126–127

WHAT YOU NEED
2 artichokes
Sharp knife
Green votive candles
Coordinating plate, berries,
    and small ball ornaments

HERE'S HOW
1 Wash and dry the artichokes.
2 Slice off the tops of the artichokes. Cut a hole in each artichoke to fit the votive candle.

3 Place a candle into each hole. Arrange the artichokes, berries, and small ball ornaments on the plate.

Note: Never leave burning candles unattended.

Festive Feather Trims
shown on pages 128–129

WHAT YOU NEED
for the ornament
Glass ornaments
Rubbing alcohol
Paper towel
Glass paints in gold, copper, and
    iridescent white, or acrylic paints
    with a glass primer
Paintbrushes, angle and fine point
Fine iridescent glitter
Tiny silver rhinestones
3-D paint in glittering silver
White feathers, optional

HERE'S HOW
to make the ornaments
1 Clean the painting surface of each ornament with rubbing alcohol. Let dry. Avoid touching the areas to be painted.

2 Use the designs, *opposite*, for painting inspiration. To make the tree, use the angle paintbrush and gold paint. Make a sweeping stroke for the branches starting from the outside tip of the branch sweeping inward toward the center of the tree. Let dry. Repeat this motion with the iridescent paint; while wet, sprinkle some glitter onto the painted areas. Create a star and base for the tree using a fine-point paintbrush and copper paint.
3 Glue rhinestones onto the painted tree using a small amount of 3D glittering silver paint. Let dry. Insert a white feather or two inside the ornaments if desired.

Festive Feather
Painted-Design
Ideas

5 Punch holes into the papers and bag for handles. Cut two pieces of ivory rope for handles. Thread the ropes through the holes; knot the ends to secure. Insert a jump ring through the crystal. Attach a second jump ring and connect it to the eyelet to hang the crystal.

Flowering Snowballs
shown on page 130

WHAT YOU NEED
Scissors; dried dahlias; pliers
14-inch piece of 1-inch-wide
   sheer white ribbon
Hot-glue gun and glue sticks

HERE'S HOW
1 Cut the stems from two like-size dahlias. Using pliers, carefully remove the backs so the dahlias lie as flat as possible.

2 Fold a 14-inch piece of 1-inch-wide sheer white ribbon in half. Cut a V at the ribbon ends for a decorative edge.
3 Hot-glue folded ribbon to a dahlia back, with cut ends of ribbon extended slightly below the flower. Apply more glue; attach the back of the remaining dahlia. Break off pieces of an extra dahlia; glue to fill in.

Dried Dahlia Wreath
shown on page 131

WHAT YOU NEED
Heavy crafts wire or 7-inch metal
   macramé ring
Wire cutter
Dried dahlias
Fine crafts wire
Hot-glue gun and glue sticks
24-inch piece of 1-inch-wide
   sheer white ribbon

WHAT YOU NEED
for the gift bag
Scissors; gold card stock
Ivory paper bag; ⅛-inch hole punch
⅛-inch gold scrapbook eyelet
Eyelet setter and hammer
Ivory scrapbook paper
Decorative-edge scissors, optional
Glass or acrylic paints in gold, copper,
   and iridescent white
Paintbrushes, angle and fine point
Fine iridescent glitter
Tiny silver rhinestones
3-D paint in glittering silver
Double-sided tape; ivory rope trim
Gold jump rings; teardrop crystal
Long-nose pliers

HERE'S HOW
to make the gift bag
1 Cut a triangular piece of gold card stock to fit the front of the gift bag. Include a 1-inch lip to fold down and fit inside of the bag. Punch a hole at the bottom point of the paper and insert a gold eyelet using an eyelet setter and hammer.
2 Cut a piece of ivory paper to lay on top of the gold paper with a ¼-inch margin. Trim the edges of the ivory paper with decorative-edge scissors if desired.
3 Paint the tree or other design from *page 135* on the ivory paper as was done on the glass ornaments, *page 134*. Let dry.
4 Tape the ivory paper to the gold paper and then to the bag.

stick and immediately begin dripping the wax onto the petals of a pinecone. Work quickly and on one section at a time. Let the wax cool and set before working on a new section of the pinecone. Blow out the sealing stick when not in use. If desired, use multiple colors of wax on a pinecone.

3 Drill a hole in the bottom center of each pinecone. Thread a rondelle bead onto each eye screw and twist into pinecone.

4 Cut a 10- to 12-inch length of narrow ribbon or cord for each pinecone; thread through eye screw and knot ends. Thread a 12-inch length of green ribbon through narrow ribbon loops, tie, and curl ends.

HERE'S HOW

1 To make the wreath base, form a 7-inch diameter ring from wire or use a purchased metal macramé ring.

2 Cut the wire stems from about 10 dried dahlias; position dahlias around ring to test arrangement. When the desired look is achieved, insert a small piece of fine wire into each dahlia base and twist around the stem and wire ring to attach. Use hot glue to secure the dahlias to the ring. Break off pieces of an extra dahlia and glue to fill in gaps as needed.

3 Loop sheer white ribbon around the wreath. Knot or tie the ribbon ends into a bow to hang.

HERE'S HOW

1 On a surface protected with waxed paper, spread out the bags of potpourri. Separate the pieces by color and by size, sorting those which are small enough to fit through the neck of the glass ornaments.

2 Remove the metal ornament caps. Fill each ornament with potpourri. Replace ornament caps.

3 Hot-glue a few pieces of potpourri directly to and around the ornament cap.

Color-Dipped Pinecones
shown on page 133

WHAT YOU NEED
Pinecones
Wire; wire cutters
Waxed paper
Old pillar candle
Matches
Candle sealing wax sticks in
   assorted colors
Drill
Gold rondelle beads; eye screws
$1/8$-inch-wide metallic gold ribbon
   or cord
Scissors; ruler
$1/2$-inch-wide green wire-edge ribbon

HERE'S HOW

1 For each pinecone wrap wire around the bottom and form a loop in the end for hanging the pinecone in the oven. Hang the pinecones upside down from an oven rack and bake them at 200°F for 20 minutes to kill any organisms. Let the pinecones cool.

2 On a surface protected with waxed paper, light an old pillar candle to be used as a light source. Light one sealing wax

Pretty Potpourri Balls
shown on page 132

WHAT YOU NEED
Waxed paper
Small potpourri in red, green, and ivory
Clear glass ornaments
Hot-glue gun and glue sticks

Make your own handmade gifts and wraps and then present them with pride for a very special holiday tradition.

pretty
gifts & wraps

Grand Gift Boxes, *left*, make presents look
extraordinary with easy-to-find scrapbook paper
accents. Create **Classy Coasters**, *below*, and a
bowed box to hold them. So easy to make, you'll
want a set for yourself. Instructions are on *page 152*.

Whether you love to make jellies, salsas, cookie mixes, or just fill jars with purchased goodies, be sure to package them in pretty **Tied-Up-Tight Jar and Bottle Bags**. Make the size that fits your jar or bottle and present it with a smile. Instructions for making all of the jar covers are on *pages 152–153*.

Make a beautiful **Relax-in-Style Gift Set** that will be a favorite this holiday season. Make the bath salts, soap, and powder, and then present them in cellophane bags all tied up with pretty paper shred and ribbon. Instructions are on *pages 153–154*.

Adding simple snowflakes to a purchased throw will make the winter seem warmer. Present the cozy covering in a snowflake box, creating a pretty **Winter Snowflake Set** that is sure to please. Instructions for both afghan and box are on *pages 154–155*.

Make your gift **Soft and Simple,** *above,* by using fabric or textured paper. Use twisted cording to tie around the gift. Share handwriting you treasure to make **Love Letters,** *opposite,* gift wraps. Add a pretty bow to finish the look. Instructions are on *pages 155–156.*

A **Tissue Paper Treasure** and

Beautiful Berry Wrap, *both above,*

can be created in just a few minutes

using a rubber stamp and satin

ribbon. A vintage brooch pinned

to a pretty polka dot bow makes

a stunning **Jeweled Box,** *opposite.*

Instructions are on *page 156.*

Pretty beads and fine wire combine to make **Season's Glow Votives.** Put the candles in a purchased bag and add a monogram to finish the look. Instructions are on *page 156.*

Grand Gift Boxes

shown on pages 138–139

WHAT YOU NEED

Scissors
Assorted holiday papers
Colored gift boxes with lids, such as
    photo boxes
Double-sided tape
Adhesive foam dots, such as Pop Dots
Holiday stickers, optional

HERE'S HOW
to make the tree box

1 Cut triangle out of desired paper for the tree. Cut a rectangular paper shape for the tree trunk. Apply the tree trunk paper to the box lid using double-sided tape. Adhere one layer of foam dots to the back of the tree paper and apply to the box lid.
2 Cut circles of coordinating paper for the tree ornaments. Adhere one layer of foam dots to the circles and apply to the tree. Cut one larger circle for the tree topper. Adhere two layers of foam dots to the circle and apply to the top of the tree.

HERE'S HOW
to make the present box

1 Cut one piece of solid rectangular paper and adhere to the box lid with one layer of foam dots. Cut a slightly smaller piece of holiday paper and adhere to the box lid with two layers of foam dots.
2 If using holiday sticker trim, back the stickers with solid scrapbook paper. Cut sticker outline out and apply to the box lid using one layer of foam dots for the trim and two layers for the bow.

Classy Coasters

shown on page 139

WHAT YOU NEED

Fine sanding sponge
Metal candle plates
Tack cloth
Metal primer
Paintbrush
Acrylic paints in red and green
All-purpose varnish
Bubble letter stickers in red and black
Acrylic sticker tiles
Papier-mâché round box with lid
Crafts knife; ruler
Wide red ribbon

HERE'S HOW

1 Sand metal candle plate surfaces. Wipe away the dust with a tack cloth.
2 Apply one coat of metal primer. Let dry. Apply three coats of red paint in various areas of the candle plates, allowing drying time in between. Repeat this procedure for the green paint. Apply two coats of all-purpose varnish. Let dry.
3 Apply letter and tile stickers to the edges of the candle plates, spelling the desired holiday greeting or words.
4 Apply two coats of red and green paint as desired to the papier-mâché box and lid, allowing drying time in between. Let dry.
5 Using a crafts knife, cut two 1½-inch slits opposite each other on the lid, approximately ½ inch from the edge. Insert ribbon from the underside of the lid and tie a bow on the top side of the lid.

Tied-Up-Tight Jar and Bottle Bags

shown on pages 140–141

WHAT YOU NEED

6 to 8 inches of 45-inch-wide holiday or
    novelty print fabric; scissors; ruler
Matching thread
Approximately 12 inches of 1-inch-wide
    or narrower ribbon or cording
Decorative buttons, silk ribbon flowers,
    tassels, or other sew-on trims
    as desired
Sewing machine; iron; sewing needle

HERE'S HOW
to make a cuffed bag for 12-inch-tall liquor or wine bottle

1 Cut fabric 6 inches wide and the length of 45-inch-wide fabric. Fold fabric, right sides together, matching selvage edges. Using a ¼-inch seam allowance, stitch the side seams from top open edges to fold.
2 At the bottom of the bag, fold the fabric to match the seam line with the bottom fold line, creating a triangle. Stitch perpendicular to the side seam, 1½ inches from the point.
3 Turn the bag right side out.
4 To form folded facing, press under upper raw edge of bag ½ inch. Measure down 5¼ inches from top edge and fold top edge to inside. Stitch the facing close to inner pressed edge.
5 Turn bag right side out and fold top over to outside approximately 2½ inches for cuff. On outside fabric, about 1½ inches under the cuff's folded edge, tack center of

cord or ribbon to center back. Add the tassels, buttons, decorative beads, or other trims as desired to ends of ribbon or cord.
6 Insert bottle, wrap ribbon around to the front, and tie a bow.

HERE'S HOW
to make a cuffed bag for a pint jar
1 Follow the directions *above*, except use a shorter piece of fabric, 6×22 inches.
2 When making the triangle in bottom, measure in only about 1 inch from the point to stitch perpendicular to the sides.
3 After ironing top cut edge ½ inch to inside, when folding in the cuff at the top, measure down 3¼ inches to turn fabric to the inside. Sew 3 inches from top folded edge to catch the pressed raw edge of fabric.
4 Fold fabric to outside, making about a 2-inch cuff.

HERE'S HOW
to make a cuffed bag for a quart jar
1 Follow the directions *above*, except use fabric 8×37 inches.
2 When making the triangle in bottom, measure in 1½ inches from the point to stitch perpendicular to the sides.
3 After ironing top cut edge ½ inch to inside, when folding in the cuff at the top, measure down 4¼ inches to turn fabric to inside. Sew 4 inches from the top folded edge to catch the pressed raw edge of fabric.
4 Flip fabric to outside, making a cuff approximately 2 to 2½ inches.

HERE'S HOW
to make bottle/jar bags without cuffs
1 For 12-inch tall bottles cut fabric 6×40 inches. Sew as directed, *above*. Instead of folding top to inside for cuff, simply narrowly hem top edge with ¼-inch double-roll hem.
2 For pint jar cut fabric 6×22 inches. Sew as directed, *above*. Instead of folding top to inside for cuff, simply narrowly hem top edge with ¼-inch double-roll hem.
3 For quart jar cut fabric 8×28 inches. Sew as directed, *above*. Instead of folding top to inside for cuff, simply narrowly hem top edge with ¼-inch double-roll hem.

Relax-in-Style Gift Set
shown on pages 142–143

WHAT YOU NEED
for the bottle embellishment
Epoxy donut-shape stickers
Glass bottles with cork tops
Large paper clip
Wire snips
Round-nose pliers
Ruler
Small gold beads
Gold rondelle beads
24-gauge gold wire
Glass oval-shape beads
Sticker letters
Adhesive, such as Quick Grip
Clear sticker tiles for sticker letters

HERE'S HOW
1 Apply an epoxy donut-shape sticker to the top of cork. Make a hole in the center of the cork, top to bottom, using the straight end of a large paper clip.
2 Cut a 6-inch piece of gold wire. Slightly coil one end using round-nose pliers. Thread one gold bead onto coiled end and thread wire up through the cork top. Then thread one gold rondelle bead onto wire. Apply a small amount of glue underneath rondelle bead to hold in place.
3 Thread oval glass bead and a small gold bead onto wire. Cut off all but 4 inches of remaining wire. Coil remaining wire using round-nose pliers.
4 Apply stickers to exterior of bottles. Cover stickers with clear sticker tiles.

WHAT YOU NEED
for the bath salts
½ cup Epsom salts
½ cup sea salts
   (available in bath and drug stores)
2 drops green food coloring
2 drops fragrance oil
   (available in bath stores)
Bowl
Spoon
Funnel
Decorative bottle

HERE'S HOW
1 Mix all of the ingredients together in a bowl with a spoon. Blend well. Pour bath salts into a decorative bottle using a funnel. Tap the bottom of the bottle to settle the contents.

WHAT YOU NEED
for the bubble bath
½ cup distilled water
½ cup mild liquid soap
1 tablespoon glycerin
3 or more drops fragrance oil
2 drops red food coloring
1 drop blue food coloring
Bowl
Spoon
Funnel
Decorative bottle

HERE'S HOW
1 Mix all of the ingredients together in a bowl with a spoon. Blend well. Pour bubble bath into a decorative bottle using a funnel.

WHAT YOU NEED
for the body powder
½ cup baking soda
½ cup cornstarch
Bowl
Spoon
Decorative bottle
Funnel

HERE'S HOW
1 Mix together soda and cornstarch. Pour the mixture into a decorative bottle using a funnel. Gently tap the bottom of the bottle periodically to help settle the powder mixture.

Winter Snowflake Afghan
shown on page 144

WHAT YOU NEED
¼ yard each of 36-inch-wide wool felt
   in white and blue
54×60-inch purchased plaid afghan
4 yards each of 4 different blue ribbons,
   such as ¼-inch velvet, ¼-inch light
   blue grosgrain, ⅜-inch medium blue
   grosgrain, and 1-inch gray-blue
   grosgrain; scissors
Paper punch; pencil
Fusible transweb paper; iron
Novelty metallic threads
Sewing machine

HERE'S HOW
1 Topstitch two rows of ribbons horizontally and vertically along the plaid lines of the afghan, leaving a space between them.
2 Fold the fusible transweb paper in half twice. Trace the desired number and size of snowflakes, *below* and *opposite*, onto the transweb paper aligning folds. Fuse to wool felt following the manufacturer's instructions; cut out.
3 Use a paper punch to create extra holes in the snowflakes.
4 Fuse the snowflakes to the afghan. Use silver metallic thread in the top of the sewing machine and zigzag-stitch over novelty threads as desired on snowflakes, securing snowflakes to afghan.

Winter Snowflake Box
shown on page 145

WHAT YOU NEED
Scissors
Scrapbook paper with large and small
   snowflake designs

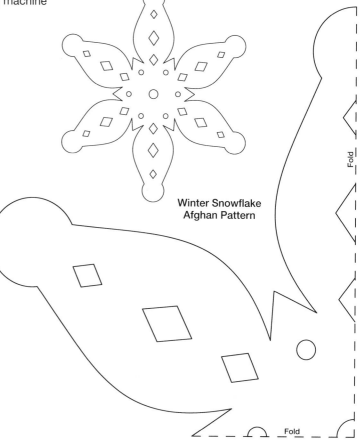

Winter Snowflake
Afghan Pattern

Fold

Fold

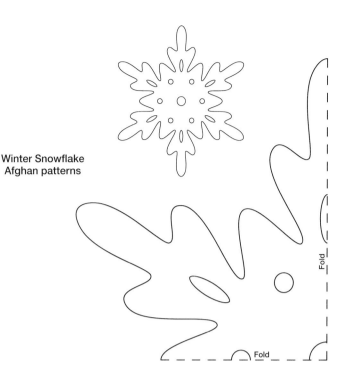

Winter Snowflake
Afghan patterns

Fold

Fold

Fold

Coordinating solid paper
Paintbrush; paper glaze
Fine white glitter; colored gift boxes
    with lids, such as photo boxes
Adhesive foam dots, such as Pop Dots
Crafts glue; small round rhinestones

HERE'S HOW

1 Cut large and small snowflake designs from scrapbook paper. Cut a middle-size snowflake out of solid-color paper following the shape of the small snowflakes. Brush the edges of the middle-size snowflakes with a mixture of paper glaze and fine glitter. Let dry.
2 Adhere one layer of foam dots to the back of the large snowflakes and apply to the box lid. Repeat this procedure with

the middle and small size snowflakes using two layers of foam dots. Glue rhinestones into the center of the small snowflakes using crafts glue. Let dry.

Soft and Simple

shown on page 146

WHAT YOU NEED

Fabric or textured paper
Twisted silver cord; scissors
Purchased ornament, trim, or
    jingle bell; gift card

HERE'S HOW

1 Wrap the gift in fabric or paper.
2 Tie the gift with cord, sliding the embellishment onto the cord before tying the bow. Tuck a gift card under the cord.

Love Letters

shown on page 147

WHAT YOU NEED

Paper in gold or white
Gift in box
Photocopies of desired handwritten
    letters or other family treasures
Shipping label
Holiday greeting stamp
Metallic gold ink pad
Pen
Upholstery cord
Tape

pretty gifts & wraps

HERE'S HOW

1 On a photocopier, arrange letters or other family memorabilia, overlapping the items as desired. Print onto 11×17 sheets of gold or white paper; wrap gift in paper.
2 Stamp a greeting onto one side of the shipping label. Sign the opposite side.
3 Tie the wrapped gift with upholstery cord, sliding the shipping label onto the cord before tying the bow.

Tissue Paper Treasure

shown on page 148

WHAT YOU NEED
Waxed paper
Tissue paper in desired color
Rubber stamp; metallic gold ink pad
Ribbon
Ornaments or greens, optional

HERE'S HOW
1 Cover work surface with waxed paper.
2 Lay the tissue paper flat on the waxed paper. Press the stamp onto the ink pad and gently press onto tissue paper. Stamp the paper until the desired look is achieved. Let dry.
3 Wrap gift with paper. Tie the package with a ribbon bow, adding an ornament or greenery sprig if desired.

Beautiful Berry Wrap

shown on page 148

WHAT YOU NEED
Box wrapped in silver or stamped paper
Fabric ribbon
Fresh berry sprig

HERE'S HOW
1 Tie a fabric bow around the wrapped box. Tuck a berry sprig under the bow.

Jeweled Box

shown on page 149

WHAT YOU NEED
Wrapped gift box
Coordinating polka-dot ribbon
Jeweled brooch

HERE'S HOW
1 Tie a fabric multiloop bow around the wrapped box. Pin the brooch in the center of the bow.

Season's Glow Votives

shown on pages 150–151

WHAT YOU NEED
Wire cutters
Medium crafting wire; yardstick
Colored glass votive candleholder with straight sides
Round-nose pliers

Small beads
Large glass bead charm
Colored microbeads or sand
Votive candle
Gift bag with gift tag
Cord
Beads with large holes
Alphabet sticker

HERE'S HOW
1 Cut a 24-inch piece of wire. Wrap the wire around the top part of the candleholder; twist wires to secure using round-nose pliers. Slide a small bead onto the short wire tail and use the pliers to coil the end so the bead stays in place.
2 Wrap the candleholder with wire, leaving a 4-inch tail. Tuck the tail twice under the last wrap to secure.
3 Bead 2-inches of the wire. Use round-nose pliers to shape the end into a loop, thread onto the bead charm, and squeeze loop closed. Add a short piece of coiled wire to the opposite end of the bead if desired.
4 Fill the bottom of the candleholder with microbeads or sand. Nestle the candle in the holder.
5 To give a candle as a gift, place the votive in a gift bag. Thread large and small beads onto three lengths of cord and tie onto the handle of the gift bag. Press an alphabet sticker initial onto the tag to personalize.

Note: Never leave burning candles unattended.

stitch diagrams

Appliqué Stitch

Backstitch

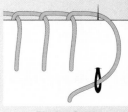

Blanket Stitch

Chain Stitch

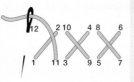

Cross-Stitch

French Knot

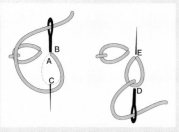

Lazy Daisy Stitch

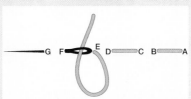

Running Stitch

Satin Stitch

Stem Stitch

Straight Stitch

Tacking Stitch

Whipstitch

Display some of your favorite handmade Christmas trims on a purchased feather wreath this holiday. Or choose a fresh or artificial wreath in the colors that compliment your holiday decorating scheme.

Christmas Feather Wreath
shown on page 3

WHAT YOU NEED
16-inch-wide purchased feather wreath with plastic foam base such as Styrofoam (available at home centers, discount stores, and floral shops)

Small crafted items or ornaments

T-pins or long straight pins

3 yards of 2-inch-wide wire-edge ribbon

16-inch piece of fine wire

Narrow gold ribbon

Scissors

HERE'S HOW
1 Lay the wreath on a table and arrange the trims as desired, alternating shapes and colors. Use the pins to first poke through the item and then into the wreath to secure it in place. Make a large bow for the wreath and wrap the fine wire around the bow to secure. Wrap the wire around the wreath to secure the bow. Trim the ends of the bow. Thread the narrow gold ribbon through an ornament with a loop top and tie at the top. Use a pin to secure the ornament under the bow.

Note: *If using a fresh or artificial wreath, items can be wired on with fine wire.*

index

index *continued*

sources

ADHESIVES
Aleenes
www.duncancrafts.com

Elmer's Glue Stick
800-849-9400
www.elmers.com

CLAY TEXTURE SHEETS
Polyform Products
1901 Estes Avenue
Elk Grove, IL 60007
www.sculpey.com

EMBOSSING METAL
American Art Clay Co., Inc.
4717 W. 16th Street
Indianapolis, IN 46222

EYELETS
Persnippity
801-523-3338
www.persnippity.com

FINISHES, PAINTS, STENCILS
Delta Technical Coatings, Inc.
2550 Pellissier Place
Whittier, CA 90601
www.deltacrafts.com

MINIATURE MARBLES
Halcraft USA, Inc.
30 West 24th Street
New York, NY 10010
212-376-1580

MOSAIC GROUT AND TILES
Clearly Mosaics—The Beadery Craft
Products
P.O. Box 178
Hope Valley, RI, 02832
401-539-2432
www.thebeadery.com

PIGMENT INK PADS
Clearsnap Inc.
Box 98
Anacortes, WA 98221
800-448-4862
www.clearsnap.com

RIBBON
Midori, Inc.
708 6th Avenue North
Seattle, WA 98109
800-659-3049
www.midoriribbon.com

RUBBER STAMPS/INK PADS
Art Impressions
800-393-2014
www.artimpressions.com

Stampin' Up!
801-601-5400
www.stampinup.com

YARN
Caron International
1481 W. 2nd Street
Washington, NC 27889
www.caron.com

Lion Brand Yarn
34 West 15th Street
New York, NY 10011
Customer service:
(800) 258-9276
www.lionbrand.com